The Foster Kid
Kid
A Success
Story

By

Jeremy Collier

THE FOSTER KID

Copyright © 2023 by Jeremy Collier

ISBN: 978-1-0882-8974-7

The views expressed in this work are solely those of the author.

To order additional copies of this book, contact:
Jeremy Collier
https://the-foster-kid.com/
JeremyCollier0205@yahoo.com

Contents

DEDICATION

I would like to dedicate this book to my wife and children. They have given my life new meaning and together we have created the family I always wanted and dreamed about.

PREFACE

Foster youth face obstacles in life that most of us could never imagine. They have to fight to be treated as normal children even though laws do not allow for it. So many foster youths will never know what a true family really is and may never know what love is. Foster youth face a lot of adversity, and the majority will never even make it to college. Of those that do make it to college, less than 3 percent will actually graduate with a degree. We, as a country, need to fight for change so that we can see improvement in these statistics and improve the lives of foster children across our nation. Looking at the overwhelming statistics concerning foster youth who have aged out of the system, it is clear that more needs to be done to ensure each of them succeeds in life. Foster youth need programs and support to help them during and after they age out or emancipate from foster care. Although there is some support out there, there is still a great deal that can be done to support the lives and futures of foster youth across the nation. You can see some of the statistics about foster youth below.

- Each year, more than 400,000 children experience foster care in the United States.
- In 2017, 9 out of every 1,000 children in the United States were determined to be victims of abuse or neglect.
- 15% of children in foster care have languished there for three or more years.

- Of children who entered foster care in 2017, 49% were five years old or younger at the time they entered the system.
- 50% will never graduate from high school or obtain GED.
- Only 15% of foster children will attend college, and fewer than 3% will earn a college degree.
- 25% of foster children experience PTSD (comparable to the rate of U.S. war veterans), and tend to suffer high rates of debilitating depression and low self-esteem.
- After "aging out" of the system, 25% of foster teens will experience homelessness at least once.

CHAPTER 1

When we were kids, we did not know what the true meaning of right and wrong was. We only knew what we have been taught by our parents and the environment they put us in. It has been debated for hundreds of years about whether or not humans are born evil or if we are influenced by society. But I ask, how can we be born corrupt, grow up in a horrible environment, and still turn out to be good person despite the odds? I am a living contradiction to the belief that we are molded by the environment around us and only the environment around us.

Some of us grow up in environments where there are drugs, abuse, and violence, and we have to learn how to react to it. Maturing at a younger age than most people, I had to basically take care of myself from the age that I could walk. I grew up in a family of eight—my mom and dad, two older brothers, two older sisters, and a younger brother. My two older brothers are Shane and Bryce; Tracy and Erica are my two sisters. John and Aaron are my two younger brothers. Aaron was not born until much later, which is why I did not count him as a part of the eight members of my family at the time.

Even before I started fending for myself, I can still remember my mom and dad hardly being around to do anything for my siblings and me. They were always out drinking at a bar or partying at home, completely oblivious to the world. It was not always just them either. They would invite a bunch of their friends over too, drinking, smoking marijuana, and sometimes taking pills. Of course, even today, they probably will not admit that any of this ever happened, but I remember, and I know the truth.

Since my parents were never home and loved to have a good time, it was nearly impossible for them to hold a job for a long period. Just thinking about it now, I cannot think of a single time when my parents actually had a job in the first place. Not having a means of income, we had to move houses a lot. This also meant that my siblings and I would have to change schools sometimes more than once a year.

Moving around all the time was never fun. We were constantly having to just pack everything up again and move because we were evicted from yet another house. Every kid hates moving to a new school, having to make new friends, and getting used to a completely new environment. Before I was in the third grade, I had experienced moving to five different school districts and elementary schools. This does not include all the houses we had moved to, which were around ten to eleven different homes. Sometimes we would only move right down the road, and other times we would completely change towns. After so many times, I started to not be fazed by it, but I would just not settle down. I felt as if I had to be prepared to pick up and leave all the time.

The first home that I can remember living in was located in Loveland, Ohio. Loveland, if you do not know, is an outlying town of Cincinnati. It was a small two-bedroom house with only one bathroom for eight of us to share. I had to resort to sleeping on the floor next to my parent's bed; I would make do without a pillow or by piling what clothes I had just for a little bit of comfort. It was like this for most of my childhood. I never had the luxury of having my own room or even my own bed. At this time, I was only at the age of about four or five. I can still remember all of my siblings fighting practically every day over the smallest of things. Living in such a small space put a lot of tension around all of us that was impossible to get rid of. The house did not have much of a yard either; our neighbor's houses were only a few feet away. There was virtually nowhere for us kids to play. Not being able to have fun and release some energy made all of us fight even more. It would not just be little yelling matches either. Shane and Bryce would end up full-on fist-fighting, while my dad would just let them keep fighting and fighting until someone would get hurt or knocked unconscious. I was probably the only person in my family that never wanted to fight. I was only five years old, and I did not interact with others all too well. So there was not really any chance for me to fight in the first place even if I did enjoy it as much as my family did.

One of the only things that were consistent in my childhood was that we always had a pet. We always had a least one dog. And once in a while, we would get a cat. The first pet I actually remember was a boxer named Lady. At that time, we also had a chow, but I do not remember what her name was. All I can recall is that she was one of the most vicious dogs that I have ever seen with my own eyes. The first indicator that we should have gotten rid of her was the fact that she did not like anyone but my mom. I do not know why she would not have liked me or my siblings, but she did not. The first incident we had with her was when one of the neighbors was in the yard and the dog went after her and bit a chunk out of her leg. Even at such a young age, I can remember it graphically. I am not exaggerating at all when I say that the chow took a bite out of the neighbor's leg; it was one of the most horrible things I have ever seen. The fear that goes through your body at such a young age is immeasurable. My imagination ran wild, and I really believed that the dog was going to come after me next. Somehow my mom was able to calm me down, and we still decided to keep the dog. I am not completely sure what happened to the girl's neighbor, but I believe she and her family moved shortly after the incident. It would have been stupid not to after what had happened.

It was around this same time when I started school. It was an intense time because I remember that I was exceedingly ill for no apparent reason. The pain was excruciating for someone at such a young age. Constantly vomiting and feeling too weak to do anything forced me to be bedridden a lot of the time. Some days would go by when I would not feel any weakness at all. But that was rarely the case. Now that I can look back on things, my parents' habits probably had a big impact on my health. Being the heavy smoker that they were, I was always exposed to secondhand smoke. I can recall gagging at the smell of cigarette smoke. In my opinion, that is one of the worst smells ever.

My parents had to take me to the doctor quite often. The biggest problem I had, had been with my ears. I had to have multiple sets of tubes that were surgically put in my ears. I remember one of the surgeries where I was told I could take the gas mask home with me. At the time, I thought it was because of how often I was there. While that was not actually the case, it was still a tiny glimmer of joy for me at the time, despite the circumstances. The doctors did not know what else was wrong with me at the time though. So, I tried to go on living like a normal kid as best I could. After a short period, I was continually getting ill again, but that was not the only thing that was happening. At what seemed like random moments, everything would go black, my hearing would fade, and my body would go completely limp. Then the next thing that I knew, I was lying on my back with people surrounding me, not knowing what was going on or what to do either. I was only five years old, and I was already having health problems that would scare an adult.

So we went to another doctor to try and see if we could figure out what was wrong with me. After several tests and blood work, the doctors found something out of the ordinary. They said that I was borderline diabetic, which I did not know the meaning of. My parents had no choice but to worry about my health at that time. From that time onward, I had to make sure I cautiously watched and monitored my blood glucose levels. The worst thing about this was that I had to prick my finger a few times a day to test my blood. I tried to avoid this as much as possible, but it was impossible to get around it completely. After all the news, I had to try and get back to what I thought to be a normal five-year-old's childhood.

After coming home from school, my older siblings would watch us younger kids. This might not have been the best thing to do, but my parents did not have much of a choice. As I said before, my siblings and I fought practically every day. I would try and stay away from all of them as much as possible and just watch television, but in such a small house, it was not possible. What I would end up doing was going outside in the small yard that we had and running around, using my imagination and acting like an airplane or anything else my young mind was able to think of. I would also go around our other neighbor's house when possible. The father over there was named Roger. I can remember him vividly because we shared birthdays, and he owned a semi, which are big trucks, to begin with, but are even bigger to a five-year-old. Running around free-spirited was fun, but since we lived directly next to a street, we had to be very careful not to run out too far away from the house. There also was a gravel driveway separating our house from Roger's house. I did not like this so much because, being a kid, I did not wear shoes as much as I should have, and walking on gravel really hurts. Of course, not wearing shoes all the time was partly because I did not always have my own pair. Well, this did not go well for me one day. I was running around outside without any shoes on once again. Roger had a porch connected to his house, but it did not have any sides to it. Being a child, I found it fun to jump off the side of the porch. One day when I was jumping off of the porch and Roger had been pulling down the driveway at the same time. I jumped at the perfect time; a second sooner and I would have been run down and probably hurt critically. Luckily for me, the only injury I obtained was when I jumped down off the porch, Roger accidentally ran my foot over. Once he saw me, he hit the brakes immediately. As he did this, his car stopped directly on top of my foot, and it was just gravel, my barefoot, and his front tire pushing down on it. I did not know how to react, so I just stood there stupefied and unable to move, partly because of fear and partly because there was a car on my foot and it was impossible to actually move. I waved Roger on as if nothing happened, and finally, my foot was free. I am not able to remember whether or not I cried over this, but I ran straight home to my mom. Instantly, I looked down and showed her what happened, and my foot was completely black and blue. Not only was my foot hurting but after my mom found out what happened, she began to start hitting me. No child should run to their mom in pain, just to be punished by getting smacked around. After being punished, I would always just keep to myself and lie down. I did not know why I was punished for something that was an accident. Living in fear of doing something wrong and getting punished for accidents is no way to live as a child.

CHAPTER 2

It was not long after I started kindergarten at Loveland Elementary School that we had to pack up and move to a different school district because we had been evicted from our house. This time, we were off to Marathon, Ohio. Unlike the last house, this one had three bedrooms, so we had about two to three of us in each room, which was not so bad. I slept on the floor next to the bed in my parents' room due to the fact that I did not have my own bed once again. The best part of this house was the yard. The yard alone was about an acre, so we had plenty of room to play around although we did not have much to play with. Being in kindergarten is already scary enough for a child. Moving to a completely different school and home just adds more to the fear. Even at such a young age, I could not wait to go to school to get away from home. After coming home from school, I would try and keep to myself and watch television and lose myself in my imagination.

On the days that I did not get to watch television, I would try and get along with my siblings and play outside. But not having many toys, we did not have much to do together. My older brother Shane was probably the only sibling I had that was never mean to me. He always liked to take things apart and put them back together or just build things from scratch. One thing he particularly liked to do was build tree houses. I believe at this time he was only at the age of twelve or thirteen.

My parents' names are Kim and James. The funny thing about living here was that our neighbors' names were Kim and James also. In their backyard, they had a large wooded area. It was in this wooded area that they gave my brother Shane permission to build one of his tree houses. The bad thing about this location was that all in the woods, the ground was like a swamp. Before I really knew what quicksand was, I assumed that the soft ground in the woods was quicksand. It was a swampy, mucky mess, and if you fell in, it was nearly impossible to climb out by yourself. To be able to get through it, Shane placed planks down with a piece of sheet metal on top to allow us to walk on them. Right in the center and the largest tree my brother could find was where he decided to start building his tree house. I never watched him build it because watching someone build something is nowhere near as fun as just using it when it is done. Once it was finished, my brother was crazy about letting people play in the tree house. He was a very possessive person. Of course, none of us cared, and we used it anyway. My little brother John and I are less than two years apart, so if I did hang around any of my siblings, it was usually him. With John at the age of four and me being six, this tree house was like a giant castle that we could go wild in. In reality, it was a pretty good tree house, but it was no castle. It had pegs nailed into the tree that we used as a ladder, which led up to the first level. This was only the first of three levels, which is why I thought it was the coolest thing at the time. My favorite part of this "castle" was a rope swing that started at the very top level, and we could use it to get from the top to the ground quickly.

As much fun as this was, it did not distract me from reality for long. But having small moments of happiness to remember helped a lot. Sometimes just a glimmer of happiness can be light to get you through a dark situation. The constant fighting between my parents was the worst. I remember some points when one of them would just leave and take three to four of the kids and not come back for a couple of days. I believe that a lot of the fighting was due to the drugs that they were using. One thing that we always had to deal with was having a bar almost directly across the street from our house. If my parents were not partying with their drug-using friends, then that was where we could find them. And if they were at the bar, they would come home completely drunk, and then we had to deal with both of them getting into fights or even taking it out on us kids. At one point, I was so mad at my parents for going to the bar every night that I walked across the street and went into the bar to find them. Obviously, this was not the best idea. After my mom took me home, I received my punishment. She took out a leather belt and just started hitting me. I can still remember not being able to sit down afterward because of the welts on my butt. What did my mom do afterward? She went right back to the bar to keep getting drunk.

There was no getting used to the problem of my parents coming home drunk every night. Even if they did not go to the bar, they would party at the house with a bunch of friends. They would blast the music to where you could not hear each other talk even if you were speaking directly into each other's ears. They would do this on a regular basis. As you can imagine, drinking was not the only activity that would take place. There were a variety of drugs that were being used also. At the time, I did not know what they were other than marijuana. Now that I am older, I realize they were also using a vast amount of pain pills and some drugs that are still unknown to me. As if my parents taking part in these activities were bad enough, they would have their psychotic, drug-addicted friends over to partake in their activities. Every time that they came over, something bad would happen. What else would you expect to form a group of people who are completely gone from a normal mindset? Saying that bad things would happen is an understatement, to say the least. The normal drunk tendencies occurred, like falling all over themselves and an unnecessary need to yell about everything. These were tolerable occurrences. But by mixing crazy people with alcohol and other drugs, everything would keep going downhill until they were all at one another's throats and threatening to kill one another. What would start out as a few friends drinking and being friendly to one another always ended up with a huge argument, and more than once, my dad had thrown people through the windows of the house before continuing the fights outside in the street. They would fight with anything that they could find, making a ridiculous fight turn into something where someone could be seriously hurt. The fight would continue until the cops were called; and at that time, my parent's friends would disperse for fear of being caught while having warrants out for their arrest.

After the cops would leave, my parents would start fighting again and blame all the events that occurred on each other. And just like any of their other fights, they would not stop until someone raised a fist and would hit the other. My dad would usually make the fight get physical first, but my mom would retaliate and hit him just as hard as he would hit her. This would keep going until one of them would leave and not return until the next day or sometimes longer. Once the parent that left returned, they would try and act like nothing happened, but you could still feel the tension in the air even though nothing was said. The week would go by, and I went to school and tried to be a normal kid. I played in the yard and in my brother's tree house. Then the weekend would come again, and the fireworks would happen all over again. The next "great" party my parents decided to hold luckily had different people than usual. So, I thought that maybe for once things will be different and no one would get hurt or start a fight. As a child in that situation, I tried to find ways of thinking my parents were going to change and care more about us than the booze or the drugs. I kept telling myself "Maybe they won't drink today" or "Maybe they won't do any drugs

今天

today." Time and time again, these just became empty wishes. No child wants to admit that their parents are a lost cause. Even when it is obvious there were not going to be any changes to come in the future, I still held hope that they would grow up and take care of the family. Hoping for a better life was all I could do though. Hope is always important to have. It shows that you will never give up and you have faith that things will get better. I always had hope, even when it looked like I would always be in a situation of abuse. Giving up is never an option.

In the house, there was a room that was used as a storage space. The room was in the hallway that connected the kitchen to the living room. It was a small room with a large storm window; there was a door that led outside and another door that was in the hallway next to the kitchen. I am not sure why we did not use the room for a bedroom, especially with how many kids there were. Even with the extra room, I was forced to sleep on the floor next to my parent's bed.

One day, I was hanging around the house, trying to escape, while my parents were partying yet again, but things did not turn out so well. My parents were doing the same thing they had done every single day for years. They had a few friends over and were smoking pot, and the music was so loud that you could not even hear yourself speak. As I was trying to stay away from my high and drunken parents and their friends, I was running around the house and ended up going into that small room by the kitchen. I shut the door behind so that I did not have to hear the music that was on full blast and was hurting my ears. I was just jumping around on the bed and trying to do anything to pass the time. That was when I decided to leave and go outside. At first, I tried the door that led directly outside, but my parents kept that door locked, and I was unable to unlock it from the inside. So naturally, I went for the door that leads into the hallway near the kitchen. As I went for the handle, I remember thinking about how loud the music was and how my ears were throbbing. I did not want to go through the door, but it was the only way out of the room. When I turned the handle, it fell off. At first, I did not think anything of it. Even at the age of six, I knew how door handles worked, so I tried to put them back on. That is when the handle on the other side fell off too. The door now had no handles, so I tried to just pull it open, but it was jammed for some reason. Beginning to get scared, I started banging on the door, hoping that someone would hear me and help me out. To no avail, I kept banging and yelling for someone, but with the noise level of the music, it was impossible for anyone to hear me. After at least forty-five minutes of yelling, I did not know what else to do. I was trapped. Finally, I decided that no matter how much trouble I would get in, there was only one way out. I had to go through the storm window. This window was unable to be opened like normal windows, so I had to break it. Not knowing what to break the window with, I decided to just kick it. I was barefoot and kicking through a large glass window. I kicked it as hard as I could, and it shattered into pieces. The drop from the window was about three or four feet, and I jumped onto the glass, cutting both of my feet. Being scared as I was, the pain did not bother me as much at first. I ran around the house, looking for my parents. They were on the front porch, screaming and yelling like madmen. When I ran up to my mom, she just brushed me off, thinking I was just wanting attention. Then I had to show her what happened before she gave me two seconds of her time to see that I was hurt. It was then that the pain from the cuts on my feet finally sank in, and I started crying. You would think that my mom would have cleaned me up and taken care of me and made sure I was all right, but she did not. She took me inside and just wiped my feet off and returned to her friends to continue the yelling and screaming. My older sisters would eventually take care of me whenever there was something wrong. They went to get something to actually clean my feet with and make sure the cuts were not too bad to where I would need to go to the hospital. Luckily for me, they were only small cuts. One of my sisters patched me up and took me up to one of the rooms upstairs away from some of the noise so that I could get some sleep. I was scared, and my mom did not seem to care. I ended up crying myself to sleep, not knowing what was going to happen the next day when my parents were hopefully going to be sober. Not knowing is one of the worst parts. I was afraid that I was going to be punished once again.

When the next day had come, I was rushed with a mix of erratic emotions and actions from my parents. My mom was generally the one who dealt the punishments to us kids, so I was more afraid to be confronted by her. At first, they made sure I was all right and let me go on my way. But after my parents looked at the damage done to the window, or at least what was left of it, their mood changed dramatically. Normally, when I knew my parents were angry, I would run and hide under a bed like every child does when they are scared, and since I never had one of my own, I would hide under my parents' bed or whichever one I could get to first. Of course, this was not a great spot to hide; my mom would just drag me out by my feet and start spanking me. This time was no different; I ran to the nearest room and hid, but it only lasted about three minutes because our house was not very large. It did not take long for my mom to find which bed I was under. As I was being pulled out from under the bed, I thought about screaming but knew it wouldn't help. Screaming out would only make my mom more furious and make the punishment last even longer, so I just gave in and came out of hiding to face my mom's wrath and feel the rings on her fingers tear across my face as she hit me back and forth. After she thought that hitting me with her hand stopped hurting as much as she would have liked, she pulled out the leather belt again.

This was extremely painful. The welts left from the belt would last for a couple of days sometimes, and then the bruises would last even longer. Not being able to sit still in school after the endless spanking from my mom raised some suspicions at times, even more so than the scrapes and bruises on my face. I would sometimes even be pulled aside and asked by teachers or counselors from the school if everything was all right at home. I would automatically lie about what happened at home because I knew that if I said something my parents would get into trouble and I would also end up being punished again by my parents. School would end up being the only place I felt truly safe, and even at such a young age, I would prove to excel at it. My siblings on the other hand did not. I believe that it was mainly due to the fact that they did not try or care about school and graduating. I used school as a way to escape, so it meant more to me than it did to everyone else. My oldest sibling, Shane, had another reason for not being able to get through school. He was in the seventh or eighth grade and he was still unable to read. I am not sure how he had made it that far without that ability. Shane is seven years older than me, and at the age of six or seven, I took it upon myself to teach him how to read. This is not how it should have been, but since I was progressing faster than my siblings, I felt it was my duty to help them out with their schooling. Being able to help him, kind of gave me a sense of pride knowing that even though I was not getting anything in return, I was helping my brother out.

Instead of taking assistance from me and actually learning the material, I would sometimes be stuck doing their homework for them. My parents did not seem to think this was a problem because they figured since I was smarter, then I should do everyone else's homework for them along with doing my own. At school, I would answer as many questions as possible; I guess it was my way of feeling special in a way. When I was in the first grade, my teacher would ask questions quite frequently to see what we already knew. I would answer nearly every single question. One day, my teacher pulled me to the side and said, "Jeremy, try not to answer so many questions. Give everyone else a chance to at least try and answer the questions." After this happened, I tried to be more subtle about being smarter than the other children my age. I believe after school that day, the teacher went to the office to discuss what was happening with the principal. Within the next week, I believe I was told that the school wanted me to have an IQ test. Surprisingly, my parents were able to be sober long enough to go to the school and meet with my teacher and the principal so they could learn about what test the school wanted to administer to me and why. For once, they seemed happy about something that I did, but I could not tell if it was sincere or not. Within the next week, I had to take the test. After taking the test and not knowing what it meant for me at the time, I returned to my normal routine of going to school and, when at home, keeping to myself and watching television, and doing everyone's homework for them. After a short amount of time, my parents received a call from the school to set up a meeting to discuss the results of my test. We went down to the school and met in the office. After speaking with my parents first, they eventually pulled me into the office and told me what was going on. It turned out that my results on the IQ test were remarkable. I tested with such a high score that the school told my parents that they felt that it would be best for me to skip up a few grades. That means I would have gone from first grade all the way to the fight or sixth grade. The school felt that it would be a good fit with how advanced my learning had been; they suggested my parents at least give it a try to see how well I could adjust to learning more advanced schoolwork. I was excited to have the chance to be learning what my older siblings were supposed to be learning, but they, unlike myself, refused to care about school. After all of the excitement, my emotions changed dramatically. The teacher and principal were happy and proud of me, but for some reason, my parents decided that they did not want to listen to the school and allow me to advance my grades. They made the choice to have me stay with the children my own age and progress at the "normal" rate. The reason they eventually tried to explain to me was that they thought that I would be picked on too much for being so much younger than the other kids I was schooling with and would be beaten up. They did not think that I was old enough to handle that situation at that time. I disagree with their decision, and even to this day, I wish I could have at least had the chance to go through it to prove that I was able to handle it, but there is no point in living in the past and holding grudges for things that I cannot and could not have controlled. Although I was not skipping grades, focusing on something that I was good at and was able to excel at without my family bringing me down gave me great joy. This helped fuel my hope that things would be better one day.

Being at the young age of only six or seven, I did not know everything that would have come along with advancing that many grades at once. So I could not fully comprehend how things would have changed for me if I would have jumped grades. After returning to the class I was supposed to be in as a first grader, everything went back to the way they were, and I was still a normal child. At least that is the way I had to make it seem so that others did not see the abuse that was occurring at home. I was still answering as many questions as my teacher could ask, but eventually, I would try and keep my mouth shut so other kids could try and answer questions too.

In the first grade, I can still remember doing some of the little arts-and-crafts projects. In our class, the teacher pushed our desks together so that they made one big table for four to five students. After doing the little projects, she would ask us to come up to her desk to show her our results. We would get into a single-file line at her desk. I waited patiently, and one by one, we would go up to the desk and show her our projects. When I was almost up, there were still a couple of others in front of me, and as you can expect with some first graders, there was a bit of pushing and jumping around. As each student kept going forward for some reason, I started getting ill. I was feeling very weak and nauseous, and it started becoming extremely hard to hold myself up. Then my vision started to fade into darkness, and then, bam, I hit the floor in the very front of the class, and before I knew it, I was waking up with my vision still blurred and a bunch of people surrounding me yelling my name to see if I was all right. I was unable to tell what was going on; after sitting up, I turned my head and was still dizzy and nauseous. Then I just turned, unable to make it to the trash can, and vomited on the floor. And of course, being only first graders, everyone was like "Gross!" I was extremely embarrassed, but there was nothing that I could do. Someone picked me up, and I was carried to the nurse's office, where I lay down to rest until my mom came to get me. I sat there for quite a while until I ended up falling asleep. It was close to the end of the day, and my mom finally showed up to take me home. While at school, she actually showed some emotion, which confused me at the time. I was afraid I was going to be yelled at for some unknown reason. She came into the nurse's office and asked if I was okay and what exactly happened. The nurse had told her what happened from what my teacher had witnessed. My mom came over to me and hugged me and walked me out to the car. After leaving the school, the mood changed to a silent chill. I was unsure how to react because my mom had just pretended to care while we were at the school, but now it seemed as if nothing happened at all and all she wanted to do was get home to "more important things." Even though my mom had only shown what seemed like true emotion at the school and then nothing when we left, the event was serious enough for her to call a doctor for yet another checkup for me. We went to the doctor, and oddly, my entire family came with us. I can still remember lying on the exam table, feeling extremely uncomfortable. I had to strip down and lie down on the paper-covered table with the bright lights above me like some kind of lab experiment with my entire family watching me. I looked down, and I do not know if they were nervous or just cruel, but my siblings were just laughing and giggling, thinking it was some kind of joke. After the doctor came in, he tried to make me comfortable about the situation, but that was nearly impossible even at that age. I did not want to be there, especially not lying there wearing nothing but my underwear with all my siblings watching. There was nothing I could do but put my head back and let the doctor examine me. I am not sure why I had to be nearly nude for an examination, but I guess he had to examine everything, which included my privates. This only made my siblings laugh even more. Luckily for me, this appointment did not last too long. After the initial examination, the doctor left, and I had to pee in a cup, and the nurse came in and took some blood. At the time, I was unable to see any good that would come from this whole ordeal. We finally got to leave and head home, but the torture was not over for me yet. The whole way home, my brothers were making fun of me and tried their best to do anything that would get me upset or make me cry. I would like to say that I was strong enough to ignore everything that they said, but I was not. My brothers knew exactly which buttons to push to make me upset the quickest. But what do you expect from kids who never had to see a punishment for the ridicule and torture that they put me through? Being bullied is never easy to take, especially when it comes from someone who is supposed to care about you. Learning to be able to get through the bullying and be able to grow from it can be life-changing. When situations like this happen, you have to learn to just take it sometimes. Reacting to the bullying can just make things worse.

I am not sure how long it took for the doctors to receive the test results back, but finally, my parents received the call. After all the humiliation with my brothers torturing me and going to the doctors, the test results did not reveal anything that we did not know already. We found out that I did not have diabetes. What we did find out is that I had issues with stabilizing my blood glucose levels. The doctors used the words borderline diabetic yet again. So my parents were told that it would be best to start monitoring it more often to try and make sure that I did not faint anymore. I have already mentioned how much fun it is to have to puncture your finger to draw blood for a glucose test; I now had to do this multiple times a day. I ended up having to do this alone without much help from my parents. The device that was used to prick my finger was able to be set at ten different levels. The device would shoot a needle out a little bit depending on the set level so that it punctured your finger enough to draw blood. Each level shot out a different length of the needle, one being the lowest and ten being the highest setting with a larger amount of the needle extending out. Once my older siblings realized this, they figure that the best use of it was to put it at the highest level and hit me with it whenever they could. They would even hold me down and do it multiple times just to see blood come out of my body. I had no way of fighting back, so I had to basically start expecting it to happen. My parents, of course, did not stop them as they should have. I do not know if was because of the drugs and alcohol or if it was just my parent's nature, but they seemed to like watching us fight and for my siblings to torture me. Sometimes they would tell my siblings to fight or try and get me to fight with my brother

John. We would be in the middle of the living room, and they would basically force me to try and fight with John since we were so close in age. I would try and get away, but I could not. Being surrounded by six other people and being directly across John, who did not mind fighting, I had no escape. My family had already influenced John into wanting to fight, and from what I could tell, he liked the fact that he could try and hurt me without getting in trouble. Instead of fighting back, I would just put my hands up to cover my face while he would try and hit me and kick at me until finally, my parents would tell him to stop. It was not as satisfying to see me cower away. But it was still enough to watch me be hurt and defenseless. I tried to avoid doing this every time, but I knew sooner or later they would force me into that situation again.

One thing that did help me have some relief from my family's "fun" with my pain was the pets that we would have. Sometimes we would have cats, chickens, and even pigs. At this time though, all we had was a dog. The dog we had at this time was a boxer that my parents named Lady. She was very loving and playful. We had a big yard, so it was easy for her to run and not have to worry about a fence. My mom loved Lady; she always loved the animals we had. At times, I could see that she even loved the pets more than she cared about me. It was like I did not exist or that the dog was her child and I was not. Like many things, I learned to cope with it and take the love of a pet and allow it to fill my heart, knowing that at least Lady would love me for who I was.

Days went by, and things were progressing as normal. But one day, we had left the dog tied up outside when we had gone out somewhere as a whole family. When we returned though, there was a surprise—Lady was missing. We asked all our neighbors, but no one had seen her. It did not seem like we had been gone for long, but still, somehow she had been taken or was let go by someone. After days of hoping that someone would find her or that she would just come home, nothing happened. She would be gone forever. Still, we do not know what happened, but there was nothing that we could do about it.

It was not long before my parents had another dog, but this time they had gotten another chow. I do not remember her name, but unlike Lady, she was a very mean animal that did not like to be played with. My mom was pretty much the only one that could pet her and be around her all the time. So I tried to avoid her as much as I could. Just like the first chow that we had, she was very aggressive and mean.

Not too long down the road, I was trying to be sociable with my brother John and actually have a relationship with one of my siblings. For the most part at that time, we got along pretty well for once. We would play near the tree house and be almost normal when my parents were not close-by. As I already mentioned, the ground all around the tree house was not the safest area. It was like quicksand; at least that was I thought it was at the time. Shane had placed wood and metal siding around so that we could walk to and from the tree house, but that did not mean it was necessarily safe. Well, after hanging out in the woods, we had to go back home to eat dinner; my brother John decided that it would be fun to start bothering me again. So he figured it would be best to just shove me into the swampy "quicksand." Everyone had already run off ahead of me, and now I was stuck, sinking into the ground. I thought that I was never going to get out of it, but luckily, I was able to reach one of the wooden planks and pull myself out and run home. Of course, when I reached the house, all my mom could see was how messy I was. Not being able to explain what happened, I was punished and spanked and hit yet again. It had been a little longer in between punishments, so I was healed up, and the spankings hurt even more. And the almost daily routine was started again. As usual, when my parents' hands stopped hurting as much as they would like, they would take the leather belt and hit me with that on my bare bottom so that I would get the full effect.

I would go to school and be uncomfortable sitting, and suspicion would arise again about what was going on at home. So yet again, I ended up having to lie about what was going on at home. After a while, I heard news that I thought was some of the best news at the time: my grandma Edith was going to come and live with us. We just called her Grandma Eedy. For once, we would be using the extra room for a bedroom, but just for my grandma.

I thought that things would be better when she moved in with us. I figured that my mom would not hit me anymore when her own mother was living with us. In some ways, I was right, but in truth, my mom would just wait until my grandma was not around to do the punishing. Since my grandma was living with us, it made it more difficult for my mom to be able to hit me and abuse me without her seeing it, so I kind of had a small break from as many spankings and punishments. With not being able to be so physically abusive, my mom was resorting to verbally abusing me. At first, it was a lot easier to just sit and hear the yelling. But when I was able to just tune my mom out, she would grab me and make sure I was listening and looking at her. Even though she was not hitting me, it was still painful to have to take. Either way, I still preferred being yelled at to the actual physical abuse. Learning to tune certain things out and not let them affect me as much help at times. But in a situation like this, it did not always work.

With my grandma around, I was able to act a bit more normal. I loved my grandma, and I knew that she loved me too. I did not have to watch everything that I did to make sure that I was not doing something wrong in front of her. But I was still cautious, knowing that my mom was around or that she was close by almost at all times. My brother Shane was very close with my grandma, and she clearly favored my brother Shane over all of us even though she never directly said that. I was used to not being a favorite, so it did not really bother me. But Shane would always say that she was only his grandma and not ours, and that bothered me more than anything. It made me feel more isolated than I already was.

Grandma Eedy was not in the best health, and that is predominantly why she was living with us at the time. She had to have an oxygen tank with her at all times, even when she was sleeping. The worst thing is that she was still smoking even though she was not supposed to be, and the dangerous part was smoking while using oxygen. Every morning when I would wake up, I would go and check to see if she was up so that I could be around her as much as possible. The amount of smoking that she did make her health much worse. And unfortunately, it would only get worse and worse. I kept up with this routine as much as possible, and one of the times, something happened that no child should ever have to see. I woke up as usual; my parents were still sleeping, so I made sure I did not wake them. I had to sneak around their bed and slip out the door. I walked down the hall and knocked on the door to see if she was awake, but there was no answer. I knocked again and again but there was still no answer. So I pushed the door open, and she was still lying in bed. I went over to her to see if she was sleeping, and she felt unusually cold. I noticed she was not breathing and immediately knew she was gone. I looked down, and there was a cigarette hole in her oxygen tube. I immediately screamed and ran back to my mom's room. Having to wake them up was a scary task for I knew they could be very cranky in the mornings. Shaking my mom and calling out her name, she eventually woke up. Immediately she yelled, "What the hell do you want?" So I told her, "Mom, I think there is something wrong with Grandma. I think that she is dead." She jumped up and yelled, "What!" She grabbed a nightgown and ran to the hallway and into my grandma's room, and she realized what I said was true. I woke my dad up, and he ran down there with her. It was a horrible sight; by this time everyone was awake, and in the hallway looking at my grandma. There is no right way to deal with this kind of situation. There was a lot of screaming and crying. My mom had no idea what to do. So, my dad, had us kids go to the neighbor's; under the situation, they did not mind taking us in. Shane was still insisting that she was his grandma and not ours. I knew he was upset, so I did not contest what he was saying.

All of us kids stayed at the neighbor's house all day while my parents were dealing with what had happened. That night, we went home to sleep, and the next couple of days were like a daze. My parents were not the same as they usually were, which was to be expected. It was a terrible situation, and no one knew what to do. It went on like this for the next couple of days as my parents now had to plan a funeral. When the day of the funeral came, my parents made us younger kids go and stay with one of their friends. I remember asking if I could go so I could say a last goodbye to Grandma, but my parents would not let me. Even though I was the one who found her, they did not want me to see my grandma like that. For once, they seemed to try and care about what was best for me at such a young age. I can still remember exactly what I was doing that day. At my parent's friend's house, all my brother John and I were able to do was watch television and play Super Nintendo. It was a weird day being able to almost enjoy ourselves under the conditions. I knew what it meant when my grandma was gone, and even though I was extremely sad, it was hard to show emotion. I knew my grandma, but I did not have the same connection that most children would have with a grandparent. As I said before, I cared a lot about my grandma, but being so young and not having that connection, I did not cry after her loss or miss her funeral. I did want to go to the funeral to say goodbye one last time though. I know now that my reaction was a little confusing. I should have cried, but it was a cluster of emotions that made the experience awkward for me; that is one of the reasons that I believe that I did not cry.

My brother John and I did not return home until late that night. It was a very confusing time because my parents were very calm and collected, at least for that night and for a short time after. There was a haze in the house, and no one knew how to go forward. It was like we thought that if we talked or did anything that there would be consequences or that it would not be right. The haze in the house did not last too long. After nearly a week, my parents returned to their usual ways of partying and drug use. I would now have to go back to my normal life of being on edge every day to make sure that I do not do anything, in particular, to set my parents off and get punished again.

Not too long after this, it was the end of the school year, and it was summer vacation. I never called it a vacation because I preferred being in school and getting away from home. When the summer came, I had to go further out of my way to avoid my siblings and to avoid my parents. There were many dramatic events that occurred at this time in my life, not just being the one to find my grandma.

My brother John and I were getting along at the time, so we were hanging out quite a bit, but unknown to me, this would end up getting him hurt and me in trouble. There was not much for us to do besides running around in the yard or watching television. John would always want to go outside and usually would end up doing something crazy like trying to jump off the top of my parents' van or jumping out of a tree. These actions luckily did not result in anyone getting hurt.

But one of the next things did. About a week prior, my parents had their friends over, and they had brought their son who was always causing trouble and trying to fight with me and John. I was used to avoiding fights, so that is exactly what I tried to do. We could not avoid trouble when he was around, so to try and get us in trouble, he decided to throw something through the window and blame it on us. At first, John and I were in trouble and were getting yelled at, but luckily, one of my sisters had seen what happened, and for once, I had someone on my side to help get me out of trouble. So we had to clean up the window and put it in the trash. My older brother Shane had to put plastic over the hole where the window was and tape the plastic down.

After my parents' friends had left, I was still expecting to get punished for the window, but surprisingly, I did not. I figured it was probably because they had so much to drink to even remember what had happened. Unfortunately, in the next few days, they were quickly reminded of the window that had been broken.

My uncle had stopped over at our house and parked his van next to the house. Right next to the van, there was the trash can that the broken glass had been placed in. Well, John and I had been outside and were trying to find something to do. For some reason, we decided to climb onto the back of my uncle's van and jump off the bumper. At first, it was fun, and we would jump off it and twist. But then I realized that there was a large piece of glass that was sticking out of the trash can. I remember telling John to watch out and not to go toward the trash cans. I thought he had heard me and listened because we had jumped away from the cans a couple of times. But then the last time that he had jumped off, he obviously did not listen to me when

I had warned him to stay away from the trash cans. He climbed up on the bumper and jumped into the air, twisting in a circle as we had done before, but he was way too close to the glass. He hit the ground, and at first, I thought he was all right and had missed the glass. I was relieved, but then I looked down, and there was a ton of blood gushing out of his leg. He looked down and immediately started screaming and ran toward the house. Even though he was screaming, he was not crying. I hurried and got my mom and dad and told them that John was hurt really bad. They had heard him scream but did not know what was wrong until I told them. They quickly grabbed my brother and put pressure on his leg and jumped into the car. I can still remember the tires squealing as they rushed to the hospital. I did not know what to do after that. I was freaked out because I saw how badly my brother's leg was cut. My parents did not return for quite some time. We were all anxious to see what had happened and how bad it really was. My brother had to get a bunch of stitches on the inside of his leg and on the outside. It turned out that the glass had cut his leg all the way to his bone. After my parents had gotten my brother comfortable in bed, they called me into their room, and I already knew what to expect. Before I was even all the way through the door, my mom grabbed my arm and hit me across the face. If she had not already had me by the arm, I probably would have fallen to the floor. She was yelling at me about letting my brother hurt himself like that, all while continuously hitting me. I did not know how long I was being hit or yelled at because, after the first five minutes of torture, it seemed as if I went numb and blacked out. I remember trying to get up after realizing the punishment was over. My parents had gone into the kitchen to start drinking and smoking pot. I crawled over to the side of my parent's bed in between their bed and the wall, which is the spot on the floor where I go to sleep. I wanted to cry out in agony, but I knew that it would only cause me to get into more trouble with my mom.

Even though my dad had never really been the one to deal with the punishments, he did not do anything to stop my mom either. Because of this, I had spent the remainder of the summer just sitting in the living room, doing absolutely nothing, at least while my parents were gone. I knew that even though I was not doing anything wrong that my siblings would inadvertently get me into trouble to avoid getting into trouble themselves. While my parents were at home, I would just lie down in my "bed," which was really just a spot on the solid floor with a rolled-up sheet as a pillow and a small blanket. This continued throughout the rest of my so-called vacation. I was afraid to do anything at all for fear of being hit once again. At one point, I remember just flinching every time someone moved too close to me.

Finally, the end of the summer came, and I was extremely glad to return to school and spend my days away from home. I was now in the second grade and still excelling in my schoolwork. Looking forward to returning to school was one thing that really helped me get through the summer. Not having to spend the entire day at home was nice.

Going to school and then coming home and trying to avoid everyone as much as possible, my days started becoming quite monotonous. The days would start really early so I could catch the bus, and school would end at around 3:30 p.m. I still remember the bus rides home that we would take mainly because they were over an hour long and I would not be home until close to five o'clock. Besides being at school, the only thing I looked forward to was trying to watch television when no one was around and when my parents were out with their friends. I would get home from school just in time to try and watch my favorite show that helped me cope with reality—Power Rangers. My siblings would make fun of me for watching it, but it was one way for me to take myself away from my normal life and pretend that nothing in my life really mattered for about thirty minutes at a time. This, of course, would only occur a couple of times a week when my parents were not home when I would get off the bus and my siblings would leave me alone, which did not happen much either.

At this point in my life, I had no other way of escaping, and time just seemed to slow down, and it made things very dreary for me. I had no imagination to help me for fear of having fun and getting into trouble with my parents again. No child should ever be afraid of their parents, especially to the point where they are afraid to be exactly what they are— a child.

I had to find many ways of getting away from my family to avoid being harassed or to avoid my parents when they were home. I was walking through the house one day when everyone was outside, and I was looking into a closet in the upstairs bedroom, and I noticed an opening in the ceiling. I decided to climb up into the closet and push through the opening, and it was an extra door into the attic. In the hallway outside of the room, there was a pull-down ladder, which was the main way to get into the attic, but I could not reach it at my age, and my parents would not have approved of my going up there. So I would use the little opening hidden in the closet to go up to the attic and hide away from everyone. A lot of the time, I would be able to stay up there without anyone knowing, and I would finally have some peace of mind, not having to worry about getting beat up by my siblings or facing more abuse from my parents.

Unfortunately, these were only short stints of tranquility, and I would have to come out of my hiding to go eat or because my parents would end up looking for me. I tried to keep the secret door to myself, but my siblings eventually found it and would do exactly what I did and use it to climb into the attic. I could no longer use it as a spot to escape. They would go up there and play around with no fear of getting into trouble. I had to hide up there without anyone knowing to make sure that I did not get caught.

This caused me to return to just sitting in the living room or on the floor in my parents' room while they were home to make sure that I did nothing to set them off. At one time, I hated when they would go out to bars or party with their friends. But I began to become fond of those times when they were not in the house, longing for a time when I was not going to have to be afraid of doing anything around them.

As much as I was longing for those times when my parents were gone, I still had to worry about my siblings. My brothers were the ones I had to worry about most. Bryce and John would push me around or purposely frighten me all the time. I would never fight back or do anything to them because I knew that I would be the one to bear the consequences from my parents.

As I had mentioned before, we always had a pet. And at this time, we still had the black chow. It was one of the meanest dogs I have ever encountered. She was only nice when my mom was around, or more precisely, she was only nice to my mom. I do not remember the dog's name because of how much I did not like her. Almost every child would love to have a pet. So when you have a pet that you cannot go to near because it is not friendly, it is a bit disheartening. At the time, there was no way of knowing just how much this would cause a problem in the near future.

Somehow, around this time, the dog had become pregnant. So she was becoming even more of an issue with us kids. When it came time for her to have the pups, my mom had put her in one of the rooms upstairs all alone so that no one would have to be around her and risk getting hurt. Her viciousness became more evident after having the pups. I was already avoiding her, but I had to completely stay away from that room because I was afraid that she might come out of the room somehow. Since my mom had given the dog the entire room, my other siblings all had to start sharing the other rooms upstairs. I, of course, was still sleeping on my parents' floor next to the bed, so I was not affected by this change. Having four siblings living in the same room escalated things, and there would be more arguments among them. I, of course, would stay away as much as possible to avoid the madness. My mom and dad would just let them fight. They would tell my brothers to just fistfight, and then they would sit back and watch.

Since my mom's dog had puppies, she would be the only one to go into the room with her to check on all of them. But one day, this changed and caused more punishment to come my way. After coming home from school one afternoon, my parents were home, and all of my siblings were outside with my parents except for my brother John. I was just walking through the house and no one was able to notice while I saw my brother heading upstairs. I did not know what he was doing, so I went after him. The door to the room with the dog and the puppies would always get jammed, but John was able to get through it. I yelled after him not to go in there because I knew how mean the dog was, but he did not listen to me. He said, "I just want to pet the puppies." I knew it was a bad idea, so I started running after him. I went for the door to the room, but I was too late. All I heard was a loud growl and a bark from the dog. I rushed through the door, and the dog had John around the throat, and he was trying to get the dog off, but she would not budge. I could already see the blood going down John's neck. I started screaming at the top of my lungs and rushed out of the room; the door got wedged, and I only could barely fit through the opening. I ran as fast as I could, still screaming for someone to come and help. They finally heard me, but I feared that it was too late. Luckily, my mom was already coming up the stairs and toward the bedroom. She kicked the door because it was wedged, and she was able to get the dog away from John. I told my dad what happened as fast as I could, and he called an ambulance. My mom had to put pressure around John's neck to try and keep it from bleeding too badly.

None of us knew how to react; we just sat there, crying and freaking out, not knowing if the ambulance would be fast enough and if my brother would be all right. Just when we thought they were going to be too late, the paramedics arrived. By this time, my mom had already brought John downstairs in her arms. The paramedics were able to keep the bleeding under control and gave him oxygen to make sure he was still able to breathe. My mom had gone in the ambulance with him while the rest of us children stayed home and waited silently. My dad had gotten in the car and followed the ambulance to the hospital.

This was by far one of the scariest moments of my life. How are you supposed to react to this? We were just kids; we did not know what to do or say. All we could do was hope that John was all right.

After what seemed like years, my parents finally called to let us know what was happening. The doctors had to perform emergency surgery and place a tube in his throat to make sure he could breathe while he was healing, but he was going to be all right. My dad had come home that night while my mom had stayed at the hospital with my brother. Finally, a few days had gone by, and John was able to return home with nothing more than a scar on his throat when he could have been dead.

I cannot even imagine what would have happened if I had not followed my brother that day. Even though I was pushed away by the rest of my family and John could be very mean to me, he was still my little brother, and I loved him. So I was relieved to know that he was going to be all right.

After all of the excitement had died down and my mom had made sure that my little brother was back to normal, I knew that I had to deal with the aftermath. My mom and dad dragged me into their bedroom and started screaming and yelling at me. They had completely blamed me for what had happened to John. Before the yelling had stopped, I could not help but start crying, and that infuriated them even more. Then, before I knew it, wham, my mom had hit me, and my ears started ringing. Then I had been hit from the other side as well. I could not tell who was hitting me because of the ringing in my ears and the tears in my eyes. I blacked out and could not tell what was happening. When I came to, I was lying on the floor where my "bed" was, and my parents were gone. I was afraid to move or even breathe. I just sat there motionless, unable to do anything until I would eventually fall asleep. My parents did not return to their beds while I was awake, so I assumed that they went out to the bar to get drunk and act like everything was normal. I could not help but think to myself, what did I do so wrong for this to happen to me? No answer would ever come, and I would just have to learn to deal with this so-called family even more.

After that night, my mom kept me home from school for the next couple of days. I assumed it was to let my bruises heal up a little bit so that when I did return to school, no one made a big deal about it. I had to lie to everyone when I went back and said that I was really sick and was throwing up.

Eventually, things seemed to go back to the normal flow of what they had been. I would just go to school and then would get off the bus and go sit by myself. The only good thing that came out of that horrible situation was that my mom had to get rid of the dog. At least, with the dog gone, there was one less thing I had to live in fear of.

Going through so much while being so young still it took a lot to stay strong and get through it. Keeping hope and faith in the future kept me from giving up. Learning to tune certain things out and not let bullying get to me as much really helped me avoid certain fights and just get through arguments without making them worse. Focusing on something that I was good at like school and also being able to help my brother learn to read helped me feel a bit of self-worth. Knowing that I had a chance to help someone made me feel needed and wanted, even if it was for just a short amount of time.

CHAPTER 3

The teacher I had at the time had a variety of books in her classroom. She would allow some of her students to take them home and read them as long as they brought them back. I started reading as much as I could. I would take home a book every single day that I could. Finally, I found a way to escape my reality. I would still be alone at home, but I had a way to pass the time. I just read book after book. And for the short run, things did not seem so bad, mainly because even when I was at home physically, I was not there mentally because I was reading and delving into the story. Of course, that did not help release the fear of punishment completely. While I was reading a book, I would make sure that I was sitting on my spot on the floor and not making noises or reading aloud.

My parents' alcohol and drug use started to escalate. There were points when days would pass and I would be unsure if they were even sober. It is crazy to think that this would be a good thing, but when they were out drinking and then came home to do drugs, they would pass out sometimes. I would have those short moments when I knew that, at least on those nights, I did not have to worry about anything because they would be completely out of it all night long.

Even though they loved to go out and party all the time, they still held parties at the house with a bunch of friends. Having the parties at home made it hard for me to escape from everyone and get some sleep. With how loud the music and the yelling between my parents and their friends would get, it was a surprise that they did not have the cops called on them—well, not for the noise levels, that is. As usual, when my parents had their parties, a fight would break out after everyone was completely drunk. While it usually started between my parents and one of their friends, more and more often it would be my parents fighting with each other. They were both psychotic and when they would fight, they would throw fists left and right. My dad did not hold back even though he was fighting a woman, and my mom would hold her ground and hit him just as hard. Eventually, one of them would pick up an object and swing it at the other's head; occasionally one of them would connect. The fights would last for hours, and all of us kids could do nothing to stop it. I did not dare try to either.

Most of the time, the fights would just come to an end, and my dad would just sleep in a different room that night. But there was one fight that escalated to the point that my mom packed up and left with three of my siblings. Still, to this day, I do not know where they had gone. So now it was just my dad, two of my siblings, and me. And believe it or not, during this stretch of a few days, my dad stayed sober the entire time. The one reason I remember is because my dad was nice to me during those short few days. For once, I almost felt safe with one of my parents. It was a new feeling for me, and I did not want it to end. But my wishes would not come true. After maybe three days, my mom and other siblings returned home, and my parents acted as if nothing had even happened. And I knew that everything was going to go right back to the way they were. I guess I at least had a few days where I was at peace, but I had to push all of that from my mind because I knew I could not hope on having it happen again anytime soon. But I could hold onto the memory of that. Holding on to the few happy moments that I had helped reinforce the hope I held for the future. I did not know when things would get better. I stayed strong in believing that they would be better eventually.

That next weekend, my parents were right back into the bar scene, drinking it up. They went right back into the erratic behaviors that they had before. This unfortunately had continued for a while, and with my parents not being able to hold jobs, there was no income between either of them to pay the bills. Because my parents were not paying the bills, the utilities were being turned off. First, it was the electricity, but that was not too bad because we had a generator. But eventually, because of not paying rent, they received an eviction notice. Even with that, we continued to live there as long as possible. Then suddenly, we were literally kicked out in the cold.

Somehow my parents had gathered enough money to pay for a couple of nights in a hotel. But they still had to figure out where we were going to go after those couple of nights were up. My sister Erica was allowed to stay at my grandparents' condo with them, Bryce went to my uncle Nate's, and Shane went to one of my other uncle's houses. We did not know what was going on; none of us had even been attending school.

The rest of us were with my parents, and we ended up having to go to a homeless shelter for the first but not the last time in my life. I can still remember almost every detail about that place. Outside, there was a small play set with a swing and a slide for children. The actual shelter looked like two trailers pushed together. When we first walked in, there were three to four long tables with chairs around them, and the room was connected to the kitchen. This would be where we would eat. Then, down the hallway were the rooms and the bathrooms. With five of us still together, we had gotten a whole room to ourselves. It was a small white room with a bunch of beds pushed together. My parents shared a bed, I was forced to share a bed with my brother John, and my other sibling slept in her own bed. I hated having to share the bed with my brother John because he loved to just keep pushing me or hitting me in the face. Even through that though, I could not help but be a little happy that I was able to sleep in a bed for once. This would become home for the next couple of months. I had not been in school for a couple of weeks, but at the time, it did not matter because it was the middle of December and schools had let out for Christmas break. We ended up having to spend Christmas at the homeless shelter. The one thing I did like about staying there was that my parents could not have the chance to abuse us as much even if they wanted to. Since other people were staying there, they would have to punish us more silently to not cause alarm. Christmas had come, and I did not expect to even get anything. I had grown accustomed to not expecting anything nice from my parents at all. But as I was going outside with my brother to play on the swings, I noticed a car pull up. In the trunk of the car, there were a bunch of wrapped presents. I saw my name on a couple of them and was ecstatic. I knew they were not from my parents and that they were from those who ran the shelter. I had to act like I did not see anything, but it did not matter because Christmas had finally arrived. The lady who had run the shelter had someone dress up as Santa Claus. We got to have Christmas dinner/lunch and open gifts. I cannot think of a time that I was happier than at that moment. It was confusing because I was always expecting punishment, and now that we were in a place where that could not happen, I did not know how to feel at first. So the happiness was only short-lived because I knew that before long, things would change and we would not be at the shelter anymore.

Christmas time had come to an end, and it was time to go back to school. I had thought that I was going back to the school that I was already in, but I thought wrong. The homeless shelter was in a different school district than where our house was, so I had to be enrolled in a different school. This was now my third school, and I was not even finished with the second grade.

I did not even try to get used to the new school and make friends. With all of the changes that had been going on, I did not see a good enough reason to. A month or so later the school I was at before had made special arrangements for my siblings and me to start going to school there again. So there I was again, going through a crazy change. Unfortunately, I would never get to return to that school after that. After getting picked up from school and being back with my parents, we returned to the shelter. My parents had found a new place for us to live, but it was in a new school district. So after a few more days, we left the shelter to head to our new house. My parents had picked up my brothers and sisters from where they had been and proceeded to move into the house.

Reading helped me lose myself in my imagination. Imagining I was in a different world gave me joy. It helped me forget everything that was going on around me. The smallest things like this can help you get through some of the roughest times.

CHAPTER 4

Things were different when we moved to the new house. There was still the sharing of rooms by my siblings, but instead of my little spot on the floor next to my parent's bed, I was allowed to sleep on the living room couch. It may not have been a bed, but it was a lot better than sleeping on the floor again. I am still unsure of exactly why my parents had started letting me sleep on the couch, but I think it was because their room was a lot smaller than before. Also, being in a shelter with children, Child Protective Services was probably breathing down their throats a bit. Although this change was nice, it was probably the only good change to come out of everything.

I had now been thrust into my fourth different school before ending the second grade. This was the third school I had attended just in that year also. I can still remember my teacher's name too. Her name was Mrs. Tranter. I had been in a new classroom in the middle of February, which meant that there was not much time before the school year ended anyway. Mrs. Tranter was extremely helpful in assisting me with adjusting to being in a new school. Even with how helpful she was, it was still a big change for me. I was still resistant to trying to get to know my classmates. After the year that had just passed, who would not be hesitant to adjust to a new school? This was just at school. I had to adjust just as much to the new house. At the last house, I was able to get away from everyone, at least a bit. But at this new house, all the rooms connected right to the living room, which was where I was sleeping. The house was much smaller too. So, if my parents decided to start blaring music and partying, it was completely impossible to escape.

Like our last house, there was a little bit of a wooded area. So again, my brother Shane built himself a tree house. He was not at all willing to let anyone in it though. It was pretty cool too. The last one he built had a rope so you could climb down from the top. This one though had a slide built into it. Even though he did not like anyone else to go into his tree house, we did anyway, at least when he was not there to stop us.

Everything started to become what it used to be, and it seemed that we might stay at this house for a little while. I had finally finished the second grade, and it was time for the summer. Most kids look forward to the summer, but as I already mentioned, I looked forward to going to school. I knew that the summer was going to be horrible. Living in a smaller house and not being able to get away from my siblings was not something I was anxious to get started. But obviously, I did not have a choice in the matter.

At first, it started off as a normal summer where I would try to hide or get away from my siblings, but it would get a bit better. I cannot recall that my parents had jobs still at this point, but they were gone a lot of the time, so it was just the kids at home. This did help a little bit because John and I were actually getting along. It was probably just because it was the beginning of the summer and we had no one else to hang out with.

After a while of doing the same thing every day, the days just started to blend together. Even being around John, we did not do anything. There was not much for us to do. Our days were mainly comprised of just walking around the house or in the woods while my parents were out. Separate from the house, there was a garage that looked like an old barn. Half of it was torn down and just in a pile of wood.

But the other half was still intact. It had stairs that led to a loft-like area. I was not supposed to be going in the garage because of how dangerous it was, but with my parents gone, I did not care. This was mainly because there was nothing to do, so John and I would use this as our own little tree house, and I would use it to get away when my brothers were being particularly cruel.

Bryce was usually the one to go out of his way to be cruel to me. Most of the time, he would either just say something mean to me or just push me around a little bit. I did not mind it most of the time. Well, I tolerated it at least. There came a point when I just stopped caring about how my siblings treated me. I knew that there was nothing I could do to stop what they were doing or to change it. And it was hopeless to try and get my parents to do anything about it. Shane was around fifteen at this point, and surprisingly, he started to be more mature. But he started to not be around a lot just like my parents though. He had stopped going to school, and not long after turning fifteen, he started going to work with my uncle and built houses. So when he was coming home, he was too tired to fight with anyone anyway.

Even though usually Bryce would only be a jerk directly toward me, there started to be times when he would do things to try and get me into trouble with my parents. One of the times, he was the reason for me receiving one of the worst punishments I had experienced. My parents were home and just doing their normal routine. I was outside, trying to avoid direct contact with anyone. Bryce came up to me, and I was expecting to be hit or to hear something mean come from him. But instead, he started being nice and looked at what I was doing. At first, I did not think anything of it, but I started to warm up to him being nice to me. He asked if I wanted to hang out and walk through the woods a little bit. I had nothing to do, and I actually had an older brother trying to hang out with me, so of course I said yes. After walking into the woods a little, we stopped at a little opening that was not too far from the house. Then he pulled something out of his pocket, and I did not know what it was at first. It was a pack of cigarettes and a lighter. I thought maybe he just picked them up for my parents to hand to them or something, but I was wrong. He pulled a cigarette out and lit the end of it with the lighter. He inhaled a little of it and then told me to take some. I didn't want to, but he kept pushing me to do it. I eventually caved, and he made me take a hit of the cigarette. I immediately started coughing, and he just laughed at me. Then he was like "Ha-ha, I am going to go tell Mom and Dad." He took the cigarette and mashed it into the ground with his foot to put it out and then started running for the house. I never thought for one second that the whole stunt of being nice to me and everything was to just get me into trouble, but that is exactly what it was. I quickly started running after him, but being much bigger and older than me, he was much faster. He was already in the house when I ran up. I could hear him telling my parents that he found me smoking a cigarette in the woods. I walked in on the conversation and instantly knew that there was no way of convincing them that Bryce had just set me up and made me smoke.

They turned and looked at me, and their faces were red; I knew I was about to be punished. They pushed me into their room and slammed the door behind them. "Are you freaking kidding me," my mom said but with cuss words. I was speechless and did not know how to respond. And then she smacked me. I thought that my mom would be the one to do all the punishing, but my dad grabbed me and put me over his knee, and started spanking me with his hand. I did not give them any response. That was the wrong thing to do. Since it did not seem to hurt enough, they pulled out a leather belt. They made me pull my pants down so that my butt was showing, and my dad proceeded to hit me with the belt. Again, I gave no response. I am not sure if I had just gone numb or if I was just so angry that my older brother would do such a thing to me. Again and again, they both hit me and again I did not react. To be completely honest, I think at one point I started to giggle out of fear and anger. This was the worst thing that I could do. If you thought that a leather belt would be the worst of it, then you and I were both wrong. My mom pushed me away, stood up, and walked over to her closet. She opened the doors and pulled out a metal wire hanger. She sat back on the bed and pulled me back up, and I had to bend over her knee. Then, just like with the belt, she hit me. I immediately wished I had just even tried to fake a reaction, but it was too late. Every time she hit me, it took the breath out of me. I cried and cried, and finally, it came to an end. She yelled, "Don't you ever let me catch you smoking again." After that, she and my dad just walked out of the room and shut the door, and left me there in pain. I crawled over to the other side of the bed and just cried until I could not cry anymore.

My parents played their music as loud as possible and started drinking whiskey and beer. It was like I did not even exist anymore, and at that point, I was okay with that.

Days turned into weeks, and the summer finally came to an end. I could not have been happier to have the summer come to an end. School was finally back into full swing, and at last, I had my freedom in those short times at school for five days a week. I put everything I had into school. In third grade, it was not like there was a tremendous amount of homework, but I still tried to let school consume me.

School became an escape for me; but because of a decision made by my parents, there were times that I did not like it so much. For some reason, my parents had thought it a good idea to allow my hair to grow out very long. It came to a point where my hair had run all the way down my back. It was not a big issue at first until it started to become a problem at school. Because my hair was so long, certain kids at school started to pick on me and started calling me a girl and making fun of me any chance they could. I did not let it bother me much because I was used to ridiculing and abuse from others. Even if I did not show it, it still hurt a little bit. Being made fun of at school lasted for a while until my hair would get cut. It was still a few months before that would eventually happen though. Either way, I still preferred going to school over being at home any day.

As before, I plunged myself into school as if that was all there was that mattered. And in a way, I tried to make it so that school really was all that mattered to me. I knew that I could not be disappointed with school because it had to do with me and no one else. I was in control of something. Besides not having support from my parents and having to do my work away from everyone when I could get away from everyone at home, school was the one thing that my parents could not turn bad for me.

My parents decided to get yet another dog at this time. It was a huge Rottweiler that they named Duke. It was a lot nicer and was more loving of a dog than the chow that almost killed John, but I still did not feel completely comfortable around him. Since we did not have a fenced-in yard or a doghouse, my parents just tied Duke up outside. Eventually, we would find out that everything that they used to tie him up with was not strong enough. Every time he was tied up, he would somehow break the ropes or chains somehow. The thing that they resorted to was tying a tow chain around Duke's neck and connecting it to the conversion van that we owned. I still do not know how Duke was able to move with that kind of chain around his neck, but he did it somehow. Besides the boxer named Lady that we had, there is probably only one good memory that I have of a pet, and that was surprisingly with Duke. Over one of the weekends, my parents had left to party with their friends, so it was just us kids left at the house. One of my older siblings had untied Duke and brought him into the house. Well, we all went outside to spend the day, and we left Duke in the house. To get into the house, there were only two doors—one on the side of the house and then there was the front door. We had kept the side door locked most of the time, so we would just use the front door. After we were all outside, the door was shut behind us so the dog did not get out. I do not remember what I was doing that day, but we had all spent a few hours outside. Then we decided to finally go back into the house. I walked up to the door and tried the handle, but the door would not budge. So my older brother Shane tried but to no avail. Somehow, after we had all gone outside, Duke must have jumped up onto the door and pushed down the lever, and locked the door. We could not believe it at first, but it was the only way it could have happened. I originally thought that one of my siblings was trying to be mean and just locked the rest of us out, but after a quick glance, we were all accounted for outside. The side door was still locked, so we had to find a way to get back into the house. Luckily, after searching all of the windows that could be reached, one of them was unlocked. I had to be lifted onto someone's shoulder and had to break the screen. I climbed through the window, trying not to fall and break something, and made my way through the house. And just as we had figured, somehow the dog had jumped up and locked the door. For once, I had to laugh. Thinking about the impossibility of the dog locking us out was a good release from some of the hostility, but it happened. Other than this, I cannot remember a time when all of my siblings and I got along and just laughed about something like that.

After that day though, it was like none of that happened. It went back to being the other sibling that everyone picked on. Normally, my sisters were not the ones particularly picking on me. But a couple of times, they did pick on me but without me knowing.

At school, it was easy to brush off people making fun of my hair, but my sisters took it to a whole different level. I came home from school one day and was minding my own business. I fell asleep on the couch. I never thought that I would wake up to what I did. I woke up and did not really know what was going on. At first, I did not realize that my sisters had done something to me. The first thing that I did notice was that my hair was pulled back into a braid, but I did not really care. But then my brothers came in and immediately started laughing at me, saying, "Ha- ha, you look like a girl." I thought they were just talking about my hair and didn't really take hold of what they were saying. But it turns out they were not laughing at my hair. I went to use the bathroom, and that was when I looked in the mirror. My sisters had put makeup all over my face. I could not believe it. I immediately scrubbed it off, but my brothers did not stop calling me a girl for the rest of the day. I can look back now and not really be bothered by it, and I can just laugh about it a bit. But at the time, I felt completely humiliated. It made it harder to be around anyone, knowing that I had to deal with being treated cruelly by my brothers and my sisters now. Luckily, my parents had finally gotten me a haircut, so I did not have to face the same level of mockery as before. But being picked on was not the reason for allowing me to get a haircut.

Going on from there, the days were all the same, and time moved pretty quickly. It was already time for Christmas break. Winter was fun with the snow, but I ended up hating it. Once in a while, my parents were nice enough to take us sled riding, and it was as if we were a normal family. The worst part about this was that just when I started to think they were changing, everything would go back to normal.

Other than how my parents acted toward me during the wintertime, there was a very good reason why I did not like it. Sure, it was nice to be able to sled once in a while and throw a snowball, but along with that, I had an odd health issue that came with it. I do not know if it was the cold or my parents' past abuse, hitting me on the side of the head, or both. But after being out in the cold for a while, my ears would start to hurt and not in the way where it was just cold. We were out sledding when I started experiencing the pain I was talking about, so I put my hand up to my ears. When I pulled my hands away, they were filled with some thick warm liquid. After a quick glance, I noticed my hands were filled with blood. I do not know what caused it, but this was not the last time it would happen either.

All my parents did was wipe the blood off and continue to go on with their fun. After returning home and changing into dry clothes, I just went to bed. The next day, my parents left the house, and I decided to play outside, not thinking that my ears would have any issues again. But I was wrong. The blood started coming out of my ears once again. I went in and showed my sisters, and they helped me clean up. I never went back outside that day or at all for the rest of the winter.

One of my sisters told my parents what happened when they were finally home that night. I could not tell if they were sober enough to understand what was being said to them or even if they cared, for that matter. But the next day, they did call the doctor to try and get me in to have my ears checked out. I guess the blood coming from my ears a couple of days in a row was finally a wake-up call for them to make sure that I was all right. Plus being on food stamps and Medicaid, they had Child Protective Services looking at them under a magnifying glass sometimes. I could always tell when they were worried about the county child services coming to visit. They were unusually sober and tried to be parents.

Christmas was upon us, and this time, there was an abundance of gifts in the living room when we all woke up. I never expected to get any gifts with our living situations and how I was cared for, but we did. The only thing is that I know where some of the gifts probably came from, and they were not legally obtained. When I was fortunate enough to get new clothes or my older siblings would get clothes and I would get their old and beat-up clothes. We would go to Goodwill in Loveland, Ohio. My parents knew that they had a trailer full of merchandise locked up outside. So what did they do? They broke the lock on it and had us take stuff from the trailer. They were trying to make us into criminals already. I never took part in taking things because I knew it was wrong. But I did have to use some of the items that they took, like clothes and shoes.

Even though I knew this was how my parents had obtained probably most of the gifts, I was still kind of joyous to be able to open gifts with my siblings. After all of the abuse I had received from everyone in my family, I could not hate them. They were my family, and that was all that I knew. I may not have loved them like a normal family should love one another, but it was not in me to hate them either. No matter what happened each year, there was always one thing that I looked forward to around Christmastime, and that was going to my grandma and grandpa's house. It was one time that I knew that everything would be normal and that my parents had no choice but to be sober. Also, I knew that my grandparents would cook a good meal. Being on food stamps, my parents did not always worry about the food situation in the house. Sometimes we would not get to eat. Or when we did have food, I would have to figure things out for myself, cooking for myself or making what I could. We would end up staying pretty late at my grandparents' house. This was completely fine with me because then I could try and enjoy myself for an entire day for once.

The next couple of days went by in a kind of a daze. Nothing happened. My parents did not get completely wasted, and no one really argued. It was kind of scary because it seemed like something was just going to snap, and then who knows what would happen. In a way, I was actually right about this. New Year's had come, and of course, my parents wanted to party. They had their friends over and made sure that they had plenty of "supplies." Just from what I knew, they had beer, liquor, pills, and weed—not the best of combinations, obviously. I did everything I could to avoid being around their "fun." But since the house was quite small, it was absolutely impossible. As the night went on, the partying did not stop, but my parents began to get bored, so they started to make arguments. Then all of their friends gathered around in a circle, and they decided they wanted to watch us kids fight. I was forced into the circle with my brother John and was supposed to fight him. I, of course, just tried to stand there and protect myself, but they would just push me to try and get me to throw a punch, but I refused. John, on the other hand, did not mind entertaining them in their insane need to see violence. He would just start hitting me, and all I could do was cover my face until it ended. Finally, I was able to stop protecting myself and just went and hid somewhere in fear. My older brothers, Shane and Bryce, did not mind fighting each other either. They would both throw fists and tried to choke each other. I could not watch it, so I moved farther away in hiding. There was no way of escaping inside the house, so I snuck outside and hid inside my parents' van until the night ended. I ended up sleeping in the van without a pillow or blanket. My parents had been using the van as a place for storage and put a bunch of bags of clothes in there, so I used the cold clothes as a blanket for the night. This Christmas vacation seemed to be going great with the sledding and looking forward to Christmas day.

But it ended up being just as bad as it was good. John and I had fought again and after being beaten up I chose to sneak out to the van and sleep without heat. Of course, being the middle of winter, it was freezing.

The New Year had begun, and finally, school was back in session. Every day I became happier and happier to be back in school. It was my home, in a sense.

Everything was going as they usually did. I would go to school then come home and sit on the couch and read or just do what I could to be alone. Neither was ever an easy task. All I wanted was to be able to relax around my family, but they made that impossible. But I just had to try and ignore their cruel bantering and general annoyances to avoid having any chance of getting into trouble with my parents.

Another month had gone by, and I somehow had managed to avoid a single time when I was hit by my mom and dad or even one of my siblings. Not giving my siblings a response when they tried to annoy me actually paid off for a short time.

It was in the middle of February and we managed to stay at this house for an entire year, and I was almost completely adjusted and settled in. I was still afraid to be too comfortable because of how much we had moved already. Then we were hit with another eviction notice. I can honestly say I was not surprised. Though I am surprised that my parents have always been able to find another place to live in even with all of the evictions they have had.

I hated putting my trust in my siblings and family when they started being nice to me again. And oftentimes it blew up in my face like when my brothers purposely would get me into trouble. But just because trusting them turned out to be a bad idea did not mean I should just give up on trusting people. There will always be times in life when you trust someone you should not, but you just have to learn from the situation and grow as a person. You should never just give up on trusting others. You have to be willing to build trust in others, or how else will you be able to build good relationships.

CHAPTER 5

My parents sent us to school the next day, and they had no choice but to go look for a new place to live in. By the end of the day, they actually found something. It was probably thirty-five minutes, maybe longer, away from where we lived then. That day, they picked us up from school and took everyone to see where we were going to be living. It felt like it took forever to get there, and then when we pulled up, I realized that the closest neighbor was at least a mile away. It was a small white two-bedroom house surrounded by woods and fields. It had no driveway, but you could see what they used as a driveway because there was a worn path that you could tell was from a car. Also, there was a path out to a barn that I assumed the previous owners had used as a garage. We drove up as close as we could to the door and proceeded to go into the house. The only door there went straight into the kitchen with the only bathroom in the house right behind the front door.

There was a doorway that led into the living room and through a hallway that led to a staircase and the master bedroom. Also, there was one room upstairs and a loft, but the loft had to be used as a third bedroom. As soon as we walked into the house, there was immediately a look of shock on all our faces. At first, we thought it was just the smell, but then once we looked into the living room, there was a pile of trash that was about two feet high and covered the entire floor throughout the whole house. It was one of the most grotesque things I may have ever seen. Even after seeing it, my parents had still decided to move in, but first, of course, we had to clean it. While we were homeless and having to clean the new house before moving in, we ended up having to stay at one of the hotels nearby. The next day, we went straight to cleaning the house. It was extremely hard to stand the smell while cleaning the house, but we had no choice in the matter. Literally, we had to shovel the garbage out of the house. And it turned out to not just be garbage; there were mice and even dead animals. Also, the people that had owned the home or rented the home before we had a fascination with skulls, particularly animal skulls. After seeing all of this, I absolutely did not want to live there, but at least we would not be living in a hotel.

It took a few days just to clear out all of the trash before it was even possible to start to sanitize everything. I have to say, it was the hardest I have ever seen my parents work at anything. It was surprising to see them work so hard, but I knew that could not expect that hard to keep coming. After cleaning, we had to start moving furniture into the house. Only eight years old, and there was only so much help that I could give. But I knew if I did not help, I would be in trouble, and the quicker we moved the stuff in, the less we would have to stay at the hotel. I did everything I could to help move boxes and the light things that I could actually lift. Finally, after about a week, all of the cleaning and moving were done, and we did not have to stay at the hotel anymore.

The issue now was to get enrolled in yet another school. This was my fifth school, and I was not even done with the third grade. My brother Shane had issues with his grades. He still was not a great reader, so even though he was only fifteen, my parents went and allowed him to drop out of high school. Shane loved it because, for one, he did not have to worry about school anymore, and now he was able to work full-time for my uncle. The rest of us had to start school after the weekend came to an end. I never did like having to start in a new school, especially in the middle of the year. But then again, who does?

It was a rough change; everything was different, and I had to adjust as quickly as possible. Luckily, the school that I was in was a little behind in the curriculum from my previous school, so I was able to adjust to the classes pretty easily. Making new friends—well, making friends in the first place—now that was the hard part. I never did make friends very easily. Mostly it was because of having to move so much. I never saw the point when I might not see them after only a couple of months anyway. But also, I had already grown to be way more mature than most children my age, so it was hard to interact with others too.

Other than the changes with school and the new house, everything with my family was the exact same. My parents held a party to celebrate having a new place to live. Not that they ever really cared about how loud they were, but since we lived more than half a mile from our closest neighbor, they decided to be as loud as humanly possible. With all the room that we now had, they decided to start building bonfires, which would become almost a nightly ritual. They figured the bigger, the better. Being drunk and on drugs and adding that with fires was a horrible concoction waiting to explode. So that night I avoided having any contact with anyone so that I could hopefully avoid too much of the noise.

My older brothers loved to help build the fires. And living in the woods, there was plenty of kindling to go around. But they were not interested in just picking up sticks and making a fire. No, they wanted trees. So what they would do was find tall, skinny trees and climb to the very top; sometimes they probably would reach heights of thirty or more feet. Then they would just hold on and sway the trees back and forth until the tree would eventually fall, and my brothers would just hold on and hope to not get hurt. I was all for climbing trees. What child is not? But what they were doing was completely ludicrous. Of course, my parents got a kick out it and just laughed. Luckily, no one ever got seriously hurt from doing this dangerous task. What kind of parent says "Sure, son, go ahead a fall thirty free from a tree on purpose"? It is not sane, but as you can probably already tell, my parents are nowhere close to being sane.

With the space we had, my parents had friends over to party every single week. I missed the times that they had gone out to bars. I really do not know how they could even afford to get alcohol to party, but they would always figure something out. We would not even have food sometimes, but they always had their drugs and alcohol. Now that I think about it, I think they were selling their food stamps to purchase their supplies.

Just like in the last house, my mom and dad had allowed me to use the couch as a bed. It was a lot better than the floor, so I never complained. When the nights were finally over and everyone actually went to bed, I had peace. This was only because the living room was separated by a hallway from all the bedrooms. Being thankful for what you have can be hard at times. But as I said sleeping on a couch was a lot more comfortable than sleeping on the floor, so I was quite content at the time.

As I said before, there was only one bathroom in the house, but since we just moved in, we had no running water. So for the first couple of days of living there, we all had to use the restroom out in the woods. What made it worse was that we did not have any toilet paper either; fortunately, my parents were able to get the water turned on after those few days. The same went for the electricity, but we still had a generator, so not having electricity for a couple of days was easily overcome. The small things like regaining running water and not having to use the woods as a bathroom were quite fulfilling at the time. You do not realize how much we take certain things for granted until having to deal with them on a daily basis.

Time began to just fly by not because it was fun but because there was a general routine that we were back into. Just like before, I would go to school, and then I would come home and keep to myself. It was easier to be alone here; there was a barn to hide in, and if not there, I would be able to get away in the woods.

Since we had changed schools at the end of the school year and time was ticking away, it was already time for yet another summer vacation. I was now nine years old. During this summer, we had gotten to meet our neighbors and actually created a trail through the woods to their house. It was quite a walk, but we still had the chance to visit. I hated going to their house though. Frankly, their entire family scared me. This is saying a lot about how I felt about my own family. My older siblings became pretty close friends with their older children, and they would hang out quite frequently. I tended to stay by my lonesome, but occasionally, I would tag along to go over to our neighbor's house. It was kind of an odd situation with going to school because my family went to one school but our neighbors were going to a different school. The line for the school districts was right down the middle between our houses.

There literally was nothing to do to entertain myself during this time. Walking around in the woods was never a fun thing to do for me. I guess it did help me to be alone and away from my family, but it never lasted anyway, and I knew I would have to return home eventually. The days dragged on as if time was moving slower and slower every day. My parents were having more and more parties, and we all had to deal with it. Their friends were coming around more and more often, it seemed like. It actually came to a point where their friends actually moved in with us, so we had even less room than before. I had to sleep on a couch or on the floor, but when their friends moved in, a bed would "magically" appear. That was one thing that I had always dreamt of when I was a child—my own bed! Of course, I knew those dreams were just that—dreams. Eventually, the friends that had been staying with us found a camper, and instead of staying in the house, they were just outside the house. Of course, later on down the road, more friends would eventually start staying with us.

Food was already scarce enough, and having to share it with more and more people did not help at all. But what did they care? As long as they had their alcohol, marijuana, and pills, they were perfectly content with whatever living situation they had.

I cannot help but be sarcastic, but my parents did start to save money on their "supplies." Instead of purchasing marijuana, they had my older brother Shane start growing it in the backyard so they could replenish their stock whenever they wanted. I had to avoid that part of our yard because the stench was horrible. They, of course, loved it because they knew what it meant. Of course, now all of their friends had even more of a reason to hang around now.

I could not help but anxiously await the end of the summer. Or at least I yearned for a time when my parents were gone again and their friends were no longer living with us. When the day finally came that my parents were gone more often and it was just the kids left at the house, I thought for one second that I might have a little relief. I was wrong. My brothers started to pick on me even more. At first, they would just lock me into a room and barricade the door so I would just have to sit in there for hours without food or water. This was nearly a daily ritual. I was getting older and starting to get tired of the abuse. I knew that I could speak up to them because I was not nearly as afraid of them as I was of my parents. I was angry, and I showed it. I started swearing at them, and I started expressing just how tired I was of the abuse. But this just fueled them to be even crueler than before. Although my brothers did not have to wait for my parents to leave to be cruel, they chose to just sit back and wait until we were alone. Who knows where my parents were even going. I assume it was to wherever the party was that night. They must have been out of alcohol or else they might never have left.

So once my mom and dad were gone, my brothers grabbed a sleeping bag that I was using as a blanket at the time, and they forced me into it and zipped it shut. They roped it shut so that I could not wiggle free. Then, as if that was not bad enough, my older brothers proceeded to nail the sleeping bag to the top of a doorway so that I was just dangling in the air. I had no escape, and they could do whatever they wanted, whether it was just to push or even hit the side of the sleeping bag. I screamed and hollered but to no avail. There was no one that was going to help me. So I just cried because there was nothing left to do. I am unsure of just how long I was hanging there, but it felt like forever. Finally, they let me down. I had no energy to even argue with them about what they did, so I just walked away in tears. How they could be so evil so easily was one question that I would never have an answer to.

This was one of the worst summers I had ever experienced. My siblings were not done with the torture just yet. We were all outside in the yard one day, and somehow my brother Bryce had come across a BB gun. I did not think anything of it when he was just shooting at trees or cans. So I paid him no attention. I was walking through the yard, and I saw him start pumping the gun up to give it more oomph. Then he proceeded to aim the gun at me. I knew my brother was mean, but I never thought he would even think about shooting me even if it was just a BB gun. Then he pulled the trigger, and he actually shot me. It was extremely painful. It hit me in the stomach, and I was not wearing a shirt at the time. You could see where the metal BB hit because it immediately started bleeding. Instead of crying, I just started yelling at him. Why would he do such a thing? I had never done anything toward him that was even remotely cruel. After the pain had subsided, I just left and went into the woods so I could not be found. I really did hate my brother at this point, and I did not know if I would ever forgive him.

The summer was dragging on, and I was not sure how I was going to make it through the whole thing. I did not have any books that I could read, and other than watching TV there was not much I could do. Although I was happy that I had a sort of bed and we had electricity. I was still surviving and dealing with everything one day at a time. Finally, school was starting again, and there was a light at the end of the tunnel. I was not starting the fourth grade. Although I really did not have any friends, I was glad to know there was actually work to be done for school—projects, and homework. I know it is weird thinking of a child wanting to do homework, but as I mentioned before, it was the one thing that I could control in my life.

School was becoming fun; while in classes, my teachers liked to have fun with their lessons. In one of my favorite lessons, we had to build a track with foam tubes for a marble to travel in. It was exciting to have hands-on learning and have a chance to actually have fun for once. This was in the classroom though; on the playground during recess, I did not have so much fun. After lunch, we would get to go outside and run around on play sets. I tried to stay by myself most of the time but could not avoid interaction altogether. It was not that I did not want to make friends but when I did try to play with other kids, there were a couple of kids who would single me out and bully me. I remember one time, one of the bigger kids held me down while another child continued to hit me and kick me. There was nothing I could do. None of the teachers had ever seen what happened, and I never said anything either. I think that I did not say anything because I was used to not saying anything when getting abused at home. It was as if I was afraid of getting into trouble at school too. So I just kept my mouth shut.

At home, I tried to avoid abuse as much as possible. I would just try and do my homework or even pretend that I was doing homework if I thought it would get my other siblings to leave me alone. But instead, I was still being forced to do all their homework too. I could not win with them. I did not complain because I knew what might happen if I did. This continued to be the norm for the rest of the time while I was in school and living with all of them. It is kind of sad to say but I was almost glad that Shane was no longer in school, plus with my brother John only being in the second grade, there was much less homework that I would have to deal with.

As my parents continued to party and not care about anything else, we were growing even more scarce on food. Even when we had the chance to get food from the Free-store Foodbank, we had gone through all of the food. My parents were so high or drunk almost continuously that I do not even know if they were aware that we had no food. Literally, there was a time that all we had in the refrigerator was a pack of cream cheese. That was my meal for a few days straight, just licking a little bit of cream cheese. Luckily, the school knew that my family was poor, so I was allowed to have a free lunch. I began to get so hungry that I had to resort to stealing food at school. If I was getting the school pizza, I would try and stack two pieces on top of each other to make it look like there was only one piece. But I ended up getting caught. Luckily, the lunch lady did not get me in trouble; she just told me not to do it again. I knew that if my mom and dad had found out that I was stealing lunch, they would have beaten me. Needless to say, I was relieved they did not have to know.

At home, the food was the first to go, and then after not having paid the bills for a couple of months, the water and electricity had been turned off also. Eventually, my parents had been able to get back on food stamps so that we could at least have some food once in a while. But that did not solve the problem of water and electricity. To have water to drink and to take baths we had to borrow jugs of water from my parent's friends. This of course had to come from friends that were not living with us at the time. With everything turned off, their friends had all left. So that was a plus. We still had our generator, but there was the issue of getting gasoline to run it. My parents did exactly what I would have expected them to do in this situation. They packed the kids up, grabbed some gas cans, cut a water hose into a couple of different pieces, and had some of us go siphoning gasoline from random cars. It was not like my brothers and sisters were going to say no; we all needed to have electricity in our house. I am not saying it was a good thing to do, but we could not do anything about it. It was my parent's fault that we were in that situation; we just had to find a way to deal with it. Winter was coming soon, and we would have to live in a house without heat for the entire winter. To deal with this, we had to use kerosene heaters. They helped heat the house pretty well, but the smell was very strong, especially for me since I had to sleep only about seven feet away from the heater. This would prove to be a horrible idea in the future.

The winter had been pretty bad with us having to live on a generator and heating the house with a kerosene heater, but there was no other choice. Just trying to get through it without dying from the smoke from the heater was a challenge. But without the heater, we probably would have frozen to death first. Eventually, my winter break from school came to an end. I am not saying that we did not do anything at all, but I do not remember a single memory of that Christmas. As I started back to school, I was so hungry from the lack of food I considered stealing more food, but I was more afraid of getting into trouble than I was hungry. One thing that I liked about being in school during winter was that since it was so cold and there was snow on the ground, we didn't have to go outside for recess. And the best part was that I didn't have to face getting cornered and beat up again because I refused to fight back. I have never been a violent person; even when cornered and forced to defend myself, I find it hard to fight back unless I truly feel endangered.

Going to school five days a week gave me a least five meals that I knew I was going to get in a week. Even though the meals would suffice for a day, I was still extremely hungry when I went home. One meal a day is not a good enough amount for anyone. I had to get used to only eating a little because I knew there was no guarantee that I would have food on any given day when returning home from school. So I enjoyed what food I was able to get at school as much as possible. I had to live like each meal at school was truly going to be my last one. There was no way of telling what was going to happen at home. Were we going to become homeless again, or were we going to have to another school? There was no telling.

Getting through the rough times in life can be stressful, and at this time in my life, I was able to push through by focusing on the small things that most take for granted. It is hard to do, but doing this and taking everything a day at a time can help you push through.

CHAPTER 6

As time moved on, I could not help but wish that social services would just take me away from my family. I knew that they had the chance at one point, but when asked about how I liked it with my family and if I was mistreated, I had to lie. I was not even ten yet, and I was wishing that I could be taken away. It seems pretty messed up, but I knew it was what would have been best. Eventually, spring started to come, and the snow began to melt. I was able to handle going outside more often without fear of my ears bleeding.

It was still cold out in the early days of March, so my parents chose to keep using the kerosene heater in the house. When they would have friends over to party again, some of them would huddle around the heater to keep warm while downing their beers. One of these nights would turn out to be a night of a lot of pain for me. As my parents partied through the night, I did my best to stay away, but it was still cold out and even colder at night, so I had to deal with the loud music and drunkenness of everyone. I was hoping that there was something to eat in the refrigerator, but the only thing I could find was canned SPAM. Even with how horrible that stuff tasted, it tasted good to me after having starved so much. After eating, my brother John was around and thought it would be fun to pick a fight with me. I do not know if it was just to give my parents some entertainment or to just torment me; either way, I did not like it. He started being very cruel, so I tried to get away. So he started to chase me, and I had to run through the living room, where the partying was occurring. I tried to go around everyone, but there were so many people there it was impossible. I was going to run behind one of my older cousins, but when I did, he pushed me backward. If it was on purpose, I do not know, but he bumped into me. When he hit me, I was pushed forward, and I landed on top of the kerosene heater. It was one of the most excruciating pains I have ever experienced. I just started screaming and could not move. Luckily, the kind of heater we had had a metal grate around it or else I would have landed directly on the heater itself. But the grate still reached extremely high temperatures. I do not know how long I was on top of the heater, but it had melted parts of my skin to where it began to bubble up. Someone had pulled me off it, but I do not know who. I did not have a shirt on, which was a good thing because the shirt probably would have caught on fire and burnt me even more.

My mom then grabbed me by the arm as I was crying hysterically, and she pulled me into the kitchen and sat me on a chair. I thought she was going to grab something to help with my stomach, something, anything to make the pain and burning go away. But she did nothing like that; before I knew it, she swung her hand at me and caught me in the face. She just started hitting me and smacking me. I was already in pain from the heater, my stomach was burning, and I could not bear it anymore. Then I had to face getting beaten right afterward. All I was trying to do was get away from my brother, and that is what happened.

One of my sisters had grabbed a large white T-shirt and soaked it in some cold water so that I could try and cool my stomach down. I am not sure if this was the right thing to do medically, but it was the only thing they could do to help. Someone had finally pulled my mom away from hitting me, and my dad had picked me up and carried me to the car. I do not think he was sober enough to be driving, but he had to take me to the hospital. My stomach was burning still and actually heated up the wet shirt I was using to cool it down, so every couple of minutes, I had to hold the shirt out the window to cool it back on. I had to keep doing this all the way to the hospital.

Finally, we arrived at the emergency room and rushed inside. They took me straight back to a room and laid me down in a bed. A nurse had given me something to help ease the pain, but I was not able to have anything else for the burning in my stomach yet. I was happy that the doctor had not taken long to come in. I had sustained third-degree burns all over my stomach. After cleaning everything without irritating the burns too much, we had to discuss what to do with the blistered skin that covered a lot of my stomach. There were two options. The first option was to slowly remove the blistered parts, which would be very painful and would cause more scarring. The second option was to make sure that I applied an antibiotic ointment onto my stomach every day, and I would have to make sure that I used 100 percent cotton sheets or covers and shirts. My dad thankfully told them we would go with the second option.

It was rough having to put the ointment on myself every day, and I had to be careful not to hurt myself while doing it. My sisters were willing to help a little when I needed it, but that was the extent of the help that I received. My mom did make sure that my shirts and the sheets I used for blankets were 100 percent cotton. I still do not really know why everything had to be cotton, but I trusted what the doctor said. When I returned to school, I had to be extra careful because it was crowded on the school bus, and it was very easy to just be bumped into by someone at school. It took quite a long time before I was able to stop worrying about bumping into someone or something and having to only wear certain shirts. But it was not like I had a great number of shirts. The only clothes I had were the ones that did not fit my older brothers anymore. Eventually, I was able to stop applying the ointment to my stomach, but there were still huge scars left in the shape of the metal grate that covered the kerosene heater. I made sure I never went near a kerosene heater after that day.

I am not sure who had called them, but not too long after going to the hospital for my burns, Child Protective Services had shown up at the house, and I had to talk with them. My parents were not home when they showed up, but I had to answer some questions about what had happened without saying my parents were bad people so that I did not get them in trouble. After the CPS worker finished questioning me, I had to take off my shirt so a picture of my stomach with the scars could be taken. And that was the end of it. Even after all the times that my parents had been suspected of neglect or abuse and now this, they still had gone unpunished. Nothing had come out of that visit; we were still under the care of my parents. I did not want to live in that situation any longer, but I was still afraid to say anything against my parents.

Spring had finally come, and it was nice to be able to get out of the house without being cold. Since my burns had healed up, I was able to stop being so cautious about bumping my stomach on anything. And now my siblings knew that they could start being mean to me again. They were surprisingly kind while I was healing, not that they had gone out of their way to be nice but they were not particularly cruel. Instead of being physical toward me, they decided to change their tactics and did more emotional abuse. They would do whatever they could to scare me and mess with my head. Since we lived in the middle of the woods with nothing around us for miles, it was not too hard to freak me out. One thing in particular that they liked to do was to try and make me think that demons were going to come and take me. They would walk around me and start chanting, "Demons, come out of the walls." They would just keep doing this until I would start crying. I preferred physical abuse over mental abuse. I could never escape their torture no matter what. If it was not my parents, then it was them. I can look back now and see how childish their tactics really were, but I was only ten years old at the time. Unfortunately, they were not done with torturing me. Even though it might not have been one of the scariest movies, I was extremely frightened by the movie The Blair Witch Project. It was not because it was a particularly scary movie; but because where we lived reminded me of where the movie took place. Plus my brothers liked to make me think I was going to be taken away by demons. Altogether, I was really afraid to be living in that house. Luckily for me, I would not be living in that house much longer.

Before we found out we would be moving again, my brothers and I all had decided to go to the neighbor's house for something to do. While we did this my parents were going to their friend's house, which was right across the street. My older brother Shane had convinced the neighbor's son that was around his age to take us all on a hike into the woods. After what seemed like hours of hiking, we decided to go back. Shane told us to hike back while he and the neighbor went off somewhere else. We were supposed to stay together, so I continued to go with Shane while my other brothers headed back to the house. I was behind Shane for a bit, but then he and the neighbor took off running, and I could not keep up. They were still in sight, but they were out on a road, then I saw them get into a car and take off. I was now stuck in the woods and had no idea how to get home. I picked a direction and started walking. After about an hour of walking, I was officially lost, and I had no idea what to do. I started freaking out, but I knew that the road was close, so I started going toward the road. As I had thought, the road was only about thirty yards away. Once I was on the road, I just started walking in the direction I thought was toward home. I could not even be sure that this road was the same road that I lived on, but I thought it was. Eventually, a car pulled up, and even though it was dangerous, I waved it down. There was nothing else for me to do. I had been lost for a long time and really wanted to get home. The person stopped and asked if I was all right. I was a little freaked, but I just asked if I could get a ride. This person could have easily just kidnapped me or worse. But as I said, I had no choice. I did not know where I was, and I wanted to get home. I just jumped into the car, and he started driving. I was so scared that I could not even see clearly. We passed a couple of houses, but I did not even see them. Then I realized where we were, and we were about to pass my house, so I yelled "Stop." Luckily, he did, and he let me out without any trouble. I was finally home.

I could have been killed, but since I was not hurt and the person in the car just dropped me off, I was relieved to be home and safe. My parents' friend was there just sleeping in the living room. Since I was not at the neighbor's house like I was supposed to be, I had to call my parent's friend's house. They had put my mom on the phone, and I could immediately tell that they had been smoking marijuana. Instead of telling her what happened and having to face any serious consequences, which I knew would be severe, I just told her that I came home. Eventually, they came home with all of my siblings, and I had to tell them why my brothers did not know where I was at. So I had to explain what happened and was afraid that I was going to be severely hurt soon after. I am not sure if it was because of how high they were or what but I was able to avoid punishment during this situation.

I was afraid I was going to receive some form of punishment for taking a ride from a stranger, and when it never came, I made sure that I never brought it up again. After all of the "excitement" that had been going on in the recent months, I had been hoping for a time when things would calm down and we could just get to a time when there were no problems. Obviously, this was just a dream and would remain just that. Taking a ride from a stranger was very dangerous, especially at my age. At the time it was all I could do, but thinking back on it I wish I did not take the risk. In most situations, you have to think about what can come out of your choices. I was lucky to have not been kidnapped or worse, and I was happy for being safe. Focusing on the small things was fortified in my life that day, and to this day I hold that close to me.

CHAPTER 7

It was the end of the school year, and yet another dreadful summer was coming my way. I was afraid of this summer more than the others because I did not know if we were going to have food at any given time, and I looked forward to going to school. This was especially true since I knew that at school, I was at least guaranteed one meal each day. I hated not having any control over this. The summer, unfortunately, came really quickly and with some more bad news for my family. Not only was I worried about food, but we had also been evicted from yet another house and had to find a new place to live in. My parents did not find another place to live in like they did the last time. We had to resort to living at a motel. We were not just staying there for a couple of days or anything like that; literally, we ended up living there for nearly five months. Tracy was old enough to work, so she started working at the motel we were staying at to help pay for the room. Surprisingly enough, so did my mom. My mom working, and it was a weird sight for me. I thought that our last living situation was bad enough, but this was much, much worse. Before, there was an entire house to share with seven other people, but now, all eight of us were crammed into one motel room with only two beds. John would sleep in one bed with my mom and dad, and Shane and my two sisters would share the other bed. I had to resort to sleeping exactly where I expected—on the floor between one of the beds and the wall. This space was much tighter than the last time I had to sleep like this. There was maybe a foot and a half between the bed and the wall, just enough for me to sleep there, but

I had to sleep on my side with a sheet for a blanket and a bag of clothes for a pillow. Bryce had to sleep on two chairs pushed together. So I was not the only one who had a bad sleeping arrangement. Since my mom was working now, I was able to have a little bit more freedom during this time. Really, there was not much freedom to be had though. We lived in a motel, so there was no place for me to go and enjoy myself or be alone away from my family. I did not have to worry about getting into trouble with my mom and dad as much, but I still was not happy. The one thing I did like about staying here was that we had access to a pool, the only form of enjoyment I could have in this situation.

With my mom and sister working and Shane working for my uncle, my parents did buy food more often. This was a nice change of pace. Of course, living in a room with no kitchen, all we could eat was fast food. I was afraid I would get used to eating nearly every day for once. Since there was an actual chance of some freedom when we were living there, my brother John and I had somehow befriended another boy who was living at the motel. His living situation was a bit different than ours was though. As it turned out, his mom was the manager that ran the hotel; they were allotted the manager's suite, which was basically an apartment. It actually had a kitchen and everything else you could expect in an apartment. On the days that we did not get to eat and even on the days that my parents bought food for us sometimes, the manager's son would take my brother John and I out to eat. There were plenty of restaurants within walking distance, so it made it easy to just slip away and go out to eat with him. Of course, when my parents found out, they did not mind because they did not have to buy us food since we had gotten to eat. Even though my mom was working and we were living in a motel, my mom and dad still decided to go out to the bar all the time and come back drunk. So it was impossible to be able to get sleep. Just when I was about to go to bed, they would come stumbling through the door and make a bunch of noises and be their usual obnoxious selves.

The only time that I was able to have some peace and tranquility was when my dad was gone and my mom was working. And even then, I had to worry about putting up with all my siblings. There was no more just sitting on a couch and watching television or sneaking away into an attic to get away. No, there was always someone there to bother me or push me around. The times when I would get to go swimming, were the only times at that point in my life when I knew I could be free from abuse from my family. Unfortunately, it was not because my family just decided not to abuse me physically or emotionally anymore. But it was because there was always a bunch of other people around that they did not dare cause a scene. Also, luckily enough, they were not dumb enough to cause fights in a pool where someone could easily get hurt. That normally would not stop them anyway, but since we had no place else to go, my brothers and sisters also just tried to enjoy a time when we could just go swimming and have a bit of enjoyment for once.

As I had said before, my parents had gone back to partying all the time and were spending my mom's paycheck getting drunk and stoned. This started to cause a lot of issues back at the hotel. They always had gotten into arguments when they were drunk and on drugs, and it would always become physical. Hitting each other as hard as they could and banging on things would cause a lot of noise and would wake up almost everyone in the hotel. Of course, someone would eventually call the cops on them. This happened quite a few times while we were staying there. Fortunately, they stopped causing too many scenes at the hotel so that we did not become homeless again. This, however, did not deter them from partying and their otherwise normal behavior. For quite a while, they did not have an instance where the cops needed to be called, and it was relieving. I hated having to be on edge, knowing they were out drinking. It became impossible to sleep because of the anxiety of what might happen when they came home from the bar. Were they going to fight again? Were the cops going to be called again? Was one of them going to go to jail? Were we going to become homeless again?

I could not deal with all of the commotion and the anxiety from all of these questions that hung over our heads. My parents didn't even consider what it was doing to us kids. I had to just push everything away and try to forget about all the issues that were going on and just focus on getting by each day. Living day by day is no way for a child to live, especially while having to call the floor of a hotel room home!

The summer was finally coming to an end, and I truly did not know what was going to happen with school. It was not like there were school buses that were coming to the hotel to pick us up. I do not know if my parents just did not remember or if they just did not really care, probably the latter, but we did not return to school like we were supposed to. I was supposed to start the fifth grade. It was already hard enough to deal with changing schools all of the time. But not even going to school at all really upset me. How could I get my schoolwork done and be able to pass if I was not in school? Every day, I was expecting to go back to school, but it did not happen. My parents just seemed to not worry about it. I mean, my brother Shane had already dropped out. Were we all just going to quit school now too? I did not know. Maybe it was pressure from the school or from Child Protective Services but, finally, about a month into the school year, my parents got us back in school. My dad ended up having to drive us all the way to school every day. I am not sure who among us were in school at the time. I can really only remember my brother John and I going, but I could have just forgotten. Missing a month was not ideal, but I was able to catch up with the rest of the class pretty easily. The only issue was that I had absolutely zero school supplies, which made it hard for me to do my homework. My teacher was nice enough to lend me some supplies after she had been informed of my situation. Somehow my entire class had found out about my living situation too, and it just made things worse. I was already bullied enough while in school, but now they had fuel to add to the fire. I tried really hard to ignore them all, but, especially during lunch and recess, there was no escaping the ridicule. Their words were hurtful, but I had built up tough skin and could handle it. It was not that their words did not affect me at all but it was nothing I could not put up with. Being able to have tough skin to do these types of things for anyone is a good thing. Bullying can happen to anyone, not just someone like me and the situations I was put in by my parents. Even though I was dealing pretty well with the bullying at school, it made going home to the hotel even harder.

My parents were still going out and partying all the time. So I was bullied about my situation, and then I had to go home and figure out a way to put up with all the drama that would eventually unfold. It was not like I could speak up to my parents. I knew that if I acted out in any way or spoke up to them, I would be severely punished. I even had scars from when my mom decided to use a metal hanger as her new form of punishment, so as you can expect, I just stayed silent and just hoped things would change.

Soon enough, all those hopes and dreams would come crashing down because of a particularly insane situation that my parents had gotten in. As usual, my parents had continued to go out and do their weekly, if not nightly, routine, and for what seemed like a while, they actually had not caused any drama or fights after returning from the bar.

But this was all about to change. My mom's sister and a couple of their mutual friends had all gotten together at the motel one evening before they had gone out to a bar. When they left, I had the chance to just sit and watch some television. My siblings were either outside just hanging out or lying down. So this night had already started off unusually for my family. All I did that night was stay in the room and enjoy what little amount of time I had lying down in bed. It was a Saturday night, so I knew not to expect my parents until extremely late. Time was going by pretty fast since I was watching TV, which did not happen much so I was actually enjoying myself just a little bit. I checked the time, and it was nearly 11:00 p.m. But I knew my parents would be gone until at least two in the morning. Then out of nowhere, I heard a bunch of yelling. At first, I did not think anything of it because my parents were gone. Then the yelling had gotten louder and louder. I looked out the window and realized that it was my parents and their friends. My aunt was arguing with my dad, and my mom was trying to push my dad. I did not know what was going on and thought it was just one of their normal fights, so I just tried to stay away as much as possible, knowing that the cops would be called soon and then things were just going to get worse. Then everyone just started throwing fists and hitting each other, including my parents' friends. It was getting way out of control, and I did not know how bad it was going to get. Things progressively got worse from there. I do not know what else was said or what caused this altercation in the first place. All of my siblings except for my brother Shane were around, watching everything unfold. Then I thought I heard my dad scream "I am going to kill you, you son of a b——!" Then I saw him start running toward the room, and I just got out of the way. I did not know what he was going to do or what he came to the room for. My aunt had jumped into her car and started to pull out to get away from my dad. I guess she was the one that he was threatening. My dad started ruffling through clothes and then opened up the drawers of the one dresser in the room. My aunt had still been trying to pull out of the parking lot when my dad pulled something silver out of the drawer he had just opened. That was when I realized that he had really meant it when he said he was going to kill my aunt. I was in shock and could do nothing but sit there frozen. The silver thing he had pulled out of the drawer was a gun. I do not really remember it happening, but I followed my dad as he had run back out the door and into the parking lot. He pushed my mom and then turned to face my aunt's car while she was driving away. He pulled up the gun and took aim. He yelled something, but I could not make it out, and then he pulled the trigger. Bang! The gun had gone off, and I could hear it hit the car door as my aunt was taking a turn. What was happening? I had no idea what just happened or how to react. Was my aunt hurt? Did my dad just kill someone right in front of all of us? We did not know. I ran around the corner, and my aunt was still driving away, and all I could do was hope and pray that she did not get hurt. I turned back toward the room, where everyone was at now, and then I saw my mom pull out a knife about a foot and a half long, and she started running after my dad. My dad had gotten rid of the gun already and was not running away from my mom when she started screaming and tried to stab him with the knife. I was frozen, and so was everyone else. We were in shock after seeing everything that just took place. Luckily, the cops had been called, and they were finally there. My mom and dad were unable to be found immediately; they had taken off in different directions. I guess my dad had run to a room where my brother Shane was staying with a girlfriend. After hours of questioning and trying to figure out what had taken place, my mom and dad were both arrested, and we had to figure out what was going to happen to us. Fortunately, my grandparents had allowed us to come and stay the next couple of days with them. We all had no idea how to react to what had happened. Luckily though, it turned out that nothing had happened to my aunt, and she was not harmed at all. Although she was all right, that did not change what my dad had done and what could have happened to her. Two days later, my mom was released from jail, and there were no charges against her. But of course, with the severity of my dad's actions, there was no chance for him to be released from jail. A date had been set for his hearing a couple of weeks later, so we would have to wait to find out what was going to happen to him. Even though I did not really want to be with my family, it was still hard to see my dad going through this.

After spending a couple of days with my grandparents, we had to figure out where we were going to go to live. It was already bad enough that I had missed a month of school, but now all of this happened, and not only did I have to worry about not going to school, but I also had to worry about my dad going to jail for a long time and having to only live with my mom. My mind had been racing nonstop since the night of the shooting. What was going to happen to us with all of this going on? Since we had to deal with all this and find a place to live in, my siblings had gotten split up again. Shane had gone to live with my uncle who he was working for. Bryce had gone to another one of our uncle's houses to live, and my sister Erica had been able to stay with my grandparents. She was always their favorite. So now it was just my mom, John, Tracy, and me left together. We had no place to go that first night that we were not staying at my grandparents, so we had to sleep in the car. Fortunately, one of my cousins had told my mom we could stay at his house for a little while since he had an extra room. So it was kind of like a shelter since we all had to share one room. Obviously, this was not an ideal situation, but it was all that we had at that time. You can never be prepared for everything that is thrown your way. Sometimes you have to just take each situation one at a time as it comes at you. Building a tough skin and putting up a wall around me helped me deal with the chaos at times. But you have to be careful to not push everyone away all the time. As I said before you have to be willing to trust others to be able to build meaningful relationships. I just was not in a situation where that was possible at this time in my life, but I never gave up and I never will.

CHAPTER 8

A week or two had gone by, and my dad's court hearing had finally come up. We had all gone together including my aunt who my dad had actually tried to kill. Even after what my dad had done, she never pressed charges, but that did not matter with the severity of what he did. I do not remember all the details of what happened during the trial. I just remember sitting there, waiting to hear what was going to happen. Finally, the sentencing came in, and we were going to find out what was going to happen to my dad. The judge asked my dad to stand before he read the verdict. He was sentenced to three years in prison for attempted murder. Of course, I was upset, but I knew that it was well deserved. I understood how horrible my dad's actions were and what could have come from them. He was drunk and out of his mind when he tried to shoot my aunt, but that is no excuse. There is no reason for the events to have unfolded the way that they did. I still do not know what had gone so bad at the bar to have caused my dad to go crazy and eventually try to kill my aunt. Honestly, I do not want to know.

After the trial, we just went home, and we had to digest everything that happened. It was harder on everyone else than it was on me, but I was still upset. We still had to deal with everything else in our lives though, like finding a permanent place to stay since we could not stay at my cousin's house forever.

I guess my mom had actually tried to get a spot to stay at the homeless shelter we had lived in before. She was allowed, so we had gone to stay there. We were still not back in school though, so it was hard to deal with all of the chaos. Having to spend every moment with my brother John, my sister Tracy, and my mom was like a nightmare that had come to life. I was already afraid of my mom as it was, and now there was no chance of an escape, especially with dealing with my dad being in jail. My mom had become more chaotic in her behavior, and she was putting us at risk. We had been staying at the shelter for a little while, and everything was okay, and it was calming down a bit. My mom was not supposed to be drinking or doing drugs as one of the stipulations of living at a shelter. I had expected my mom to comply since we had no other place to stay at that time, but as usual, I was wrong. She had taken us all for a ride, us all being my brother, sister, and me. We had all gone over to one of her friend's house, and they had begun to party in their usual way. By this time in my life, there was no surprise seeing her at it again, but I knew that if the shelter had found out, then we would be put on the streets. My mom did not seem to even think about that though. The night went on, and the party continued. There was a curfew at the shelter, so she had to take us back. She was now driving around under the influence of alcohol with us in the car. But common sense is not something my mom had, obviously, or else we never would have been in the situation that we were in. We drove up to the shelter, and I think we may have passed the curfew because the lady who ran the shelter was waiting for my mom outside. My mom had gotten out of the car, and she and the lady had some words. It was evident what was happening; the director of the shelter could easily tell that my mom was drunk. Even though us kids were sitting in the car, there was no choice in what had to happen. She told my mom to leave and that we were no longer welcome at the shelter.

How could my mom act like this and continue her normal ways of drinking and doing drugs while we were in this situation? She would never change; that much was certain, and I could do nothing to change that. I was stuck in this situation along with my brother and sister. Sleeping in a car was never fun, but I preferred it to the floor of a hotel room. We had to pack all that we had into big black garbage bags, and they were in the car, so it was kind of like I was sleeping on a bed. At least that was how I was able to deal with having to sleep like that. There was no way to be happy in this environment, and it took everything I had to deal with this and keep going every day. After a couple of days of staying in the car, my mom had spoken with a church nearby, and they helped us out by paying for us to stay at the hotel right next to their church, which turned out to be only about a half-mile away from the last hotel we stayed at, where the shooting and everything else went down. Of course, being in this situation and my dad being in jail, my mom did not worry about getting us back into school.

Every day my mom would make me go to the front office of the hotel and make her a couple cups of coffee. They had free coffee, and I knew that she would send me to go get the coffee for her. But if it helped me avoid abuse, then I was more than happy to oblige. Staying there was a good change, in a sense. Instead of having eight of us in one small room, there were now only four of us, so I was actually allowed to sleep in a bed for once without living in a homeless shelter. Living in a hotel was not much better than living in a shelter, and in some ways, it was worse. At least at the shelter, we were guaranteed three meals a day. There was no guarantee that we were going to eat at all staying at the hotel even with the help of the church; they could only do so much. Plus it was not like my mom could continue to work at the other hotel, so there was still zero income. Not having any money makes it pretty hard to buy food. Even with not having money to buy food, my mom still figured out a way to afford to go out to the bar with her friends still. As I said before, there was no changing my mom's behavior. If she was not going to change after all the times of being homeless and without food and after my dad shot a gun at her sister, then my mom was a lost cause.

With only three of us kids staying there while my mom was out drinking with friends, it was almost peaceful. I was able to relax a bit and watch TV. But I still had to worry a little because I knew what was going to happen when my mom returned. I was prepared for being abused again, but I always held hope that this night might be different. Holding on to a small glimmer of hope can sometimes get you through the worst of situations. My mom had gone out with her friends one day, and we had to figure out how to find food to eat. It had already been a couple of days since the last time I actually had a meal. So when my mom had gone out, I had walked up to a gas station that was about a hundred yards away. I was so hungry that I had to do whatever I could to eat. I walked into the gas station and tried to act like I was just looking around, and then I just grabbed what I could and walked out the door. I had to eat the food as quickly as possible so that I could hide the fact that I took it and so my mom did not find out what I did because I knew that I would be severely punished.

After returning to the hotel room, it turned out that my brother Bryce had been there. He and one of my cousins had stolen some bikes from Goodwill and wanted to show us what they had gotten. I am not even sure how they were able to know where we were since they had lived almost an hour away, but I did not worry about it at that time. Bryce had ended up staying with us, and then there were five of us. I do not know if my mom had sold drugs or what, but she had some money and actually bought some food for once. We had enjoyed pizza for a dinner one night, and it tasted amazing. It was probably just the fact that I was so hungry and was not eating much, but I still enjoyed having what we considered real food for once.

My mom had one of her friends over that night at the hotel too, but she surprisingly did not party as I had expected. The next day was different though and would end up changing our lives forever. As if our lives had not been all over the place already, my mom decided to make things even worse. The day started off as it normally did with my mom making me get her a couple cups of coffee from the front office, but since her friend was there, I had to get an extra one for her. I would sometimes sneak a cup for myself; it was the only way I could get something other than faucet water from the bathroom in the hotel room. I do not remember if I had been able to eat that day or not, but the day just seemed to drag on and on. Finally, that night had come, and my mom had told us that she was heading out with her friend that had stayed with us that night, and they were going to meet up with some others. I did not think much of it, but I had always stayed up late to wait for when she was coming home. She had acted like everything was normal when she left, so there was no way of telling her that she was going to do something horrible that night. I had stayed up all night watching TV with my siblings and just tried to pass the time in any way that we could.

Being awake when my mom came back made it easier to deal with the drunkenness. I hated being woken up by her stumbling through the door or yelling out something stupid, so I chose to just wait up every time she left. That night was no different; we were just watching TV and trying to get along. My brother Bryce was unusually kind to me, and it was nice. It was getting extremely late, and everyone except for me had fallen asleep. It was close to 3:00 a.m., but I stayed up because I knew my mom would be home soon even though it had already been a little later than normal. Instead of just going to sleep, I decided to stay up and keep waiting and waiting. It must have been close to 5:30 a.m. or 6:00 a.m., and my mom had not returned yet, so I figured she did not want to drive and just stayed at her friend's house, so I finally had gone to sleep.

At about 8:30 a.m., someone had come knocking on the door, and I had woken up extremely tired. But what else could you expect when you only get two to three hours of sleep? I looked around the room and realized that my mom was not there still. I went to the door and opened it, and it had been one of the workers at the front office of the hotel. She asked for my sister since she was the oldest one of us at the hotel. It turned out that my mom had called and asked to speak to one of us. We had just expected to hear that she was going to be back soon and say that she had just stayed at her friend's house as I had expected. But we were completely wrong. There was no way we could have guessed what my mom was going to say to us when we had put the phone up to our ears and said hello. My sister Tracy and I had both gone to answer the phone and no one else because we figured we would just let them sleep. Tracy held the phone up to her ear, and I put my head next to hers so I could hear what my mom was saying.

Tracy said, "Hello."

I heard my mom's voice on the other end. "Tracy, it's Mom. Are you guys doing okay?"

My mom never asked how all of us were, so I was already questioning the call.

Tracy replied, "We are fine, but where are you at? When are you coming back to the hotel?"

Then my mom hit us with the news that no one saw coming.

"Well, Tracy, that's the problem. I am not coming back."

"What do you mean? Are you in jail or something?"

"No, I am not in jail. I am just not coming back. I am in Oklahoma, and I am heading to California. I am not coming back. You guys are on your own now. I am sorry, but this is goodbye."

What the hell was going on? Sorry for my language, but that is exactly what I was thinking at the time. Was my mom serious? Had she really just abandoned us? Tracy started crying hysterically, and I did not know what to do. I was in shock. All I could do was sit there emotionless. For what seemed like the first time, Tracy and I had just sat there hugging each other. So I asked her, "What are we going to do?"

My dad was in jail, and now my mom had abandoned us; we were alone. And it was not like she had left us with someone that could take care of us. She just left us at a hotel without any hint of what she was going to do. Fortunately though, after calming down a bit, my sister was able to remember my aunt's phone number. She was the same aunt that my dad had tried to shoot. Tracy had called her and told her what my mom had done, and she told us to just sit tight and she will figure something out. My aunt had called one of her friends that had lived close by and asked her to come and pick us up from the hotel. She was a very nice woman and gladly helped my aunt out. We had all gone back to her house and waited until my aunt came to pick us up later that night. It was a confusing moment for all of us. What had happened the night before for my mom to do this to us? That is just another question on the list of things that would never be answered by my parents. There is absolutely no reason or excuse for what my dad or my mom had done to us. And there is no reasonable answer for why they had chosen to follow the paths that led up to where we were then.

My aunt had finally shown up, and we had to go back to the hotel to pack the stuff that we had. There was not much except for some clothes. Fortunately, we had taken some of our clothes out of the car before my mom had taken off the night before. All I had of my own now was a small box of clothes; most of which did not really fit me.

Even with my mom was gone I did not feel safe and secure. There was no way of telling what would happen from here on out. But I had to hope for the best but still stay prepared for the worst just in case. It never hurts to try to be prepared for anything, and in my case, it helped because I never expected to be treated the way I should be. It is probably because of going through all of this that I overthink things even now. I would rather overthink things and be somewhat prepared than just have something thrown at me completely thrown off guard.

CHAPTER 9

We had all gone back to my aunt's house, where she agreed to let us live. Shane was still living with my uncle, and Erica was with my grandparents, so they did not have to worry about where they were going to be living. My aunt had lived in a small two-bedroom apartment with her boyfriend and her son, my cousin. Instead of just being the three of them, it became seven because of us. The four of us kids had to sleep in the living room. There was a fold-out couch, so John and Tracy were able to share that, and Bryce was able to sleep on a loveseat. I had the pleasure of sleeping on the floor once again. But this time, I had to sleep under the fold-out couch. I cannot say that this was better than sleeping in a car or a hotel because it was not. It was the most uncomfortable living situation I had experienced yet. At least the seats in the car had cushions; now I just had a small sheet for a blanket, like before, and a small pile of clothes as my pillow. It was nice of my aunt to take us in, but she did not have the space to take care of all of us.

Once things had calmed down a bit and a few days had gone by, my aunt had finally been able to get us back into school, which I was excited about. It gave me something to help get my mind off my life and the chaotic events that had taken place in the last few months. I was particularly glad to be back in school because there was lunchtime. Finally, I had the chance to have food almost on a regular basis, at least once a day for the five days of the week I was at school. My aunt had bought food while we were living there too. Unlike my mom, she actually had a job and income. The only problem was that now she had to figure out how to feed four extra mouths. So oftentimes there really would not be a lot of food. Actually, I remember a time that, instead of food, I would only get to eat ice cubes, which obviously is just water, but I had to imagine it was something else to try and help fight the groans and hunger pains of my stomach.

Being back in school really did help me deal with everything; the only problem was that I had already missed so much of the current year. It was hard to adjust with missing so much work, but I had already done a lot of the lessons I was given because I had been forced to do my older siblings' homework so much in the past. I am glad to say that my aunt had never made me do anything like that and that she was never physically abusive either, but that does not mean it was a perfect place to live in.

It was already wintertime, and now it was time for Christmas break again. It was not as hard to deal with this winter because my aunt did have some food usually, and we did not have to use kerosene heaters to stay warm. But when we had to go outside, it was a completely different story. Since we did not have much clothing, if we went outside, we had to dress in about four layers just to stay warm. The good thing though was that my ears were no longer bleeding when I went out in the snow, so I actually had the chance to enjoy winter as a child for once. I still had to fend more myself, but at least now I did not have to worry so much about being abused by my mom and dad.

Ever since my dad had gone to jail, my siblings were no longer fighting with me as much, and even less so since my mom had left us all. I was actually starting to grow close to my siblings for once, and it felt good. There was a hill right next to the apartment building, so we had the chance to go sledding and have fun. The only problem was that at the bottom of the hill, there was a group of trees and a creek, so if we got going too fast sledding down the hill, we could easily end up getting hurt, but we did not care. All we cared about was finding a way to forget what my mom had done. When it came time for Christmas, it was hard because we did not have a real Christmas. But I was happy to be spending it with the family that I still had around me. Time was going by pretty quickly, and finally, it was time to go back to school.

Around this time, it was really important that I was going to school because even though my mom had left us, she was still causing issues with my family. I thought that maybe it was just the fact that she had left us and said she was never coming back. But a week later, after coming home from school, it turned out that my mom had decided that it was time to try and step up as a mother, so she returned home from California. She wanted to try and keep a relationship with us, but I honestly did not want anything to do with her after what she did. I could not take her, trying to be a good mom, seriously. You do not abandon your child and then return after a month or two and decide to try and change what you did.

I am glad to say that there was no way that my mom was going to be taking us back. For me to even think about wanting to go back with her, she would have to prove that she really had changed and that she was not on drugs anymore. But I knew that would never happen, and a part of me was glad that she would never change. I believe it is harder to accept someone who is trying to change drastically from a horrible mom to a good mom than if she just stayed the same. Even though we were not going to be living with my mom again, my aunt wanted a break, so she allowed my mom to take us for the weekend, and we stayed at a hotel close by. After that weekend, nothing changed. She did not convince me that she was a changed person, and really, she did not even try. For the whole weekend, it was not like we sat down together and were a family again.

The weekend was over, and I returned to school and was happy to be away from my mom. I still hated her and what she had done; there is no way of forgetting that. I still do not know if I can even forgive her, and it has been more than twelve years.

I am unsure of where my mom had been staying after that or what she had been doing with her life, and frankly, I did not care. Things had been going pretty good for me, staying at my aunt's apartment, other than sleeping on the floor. Being in school, I was able to handle not eating as much at home, so I was almost happy. But just like any other time in my life, when things started to look up, everything just went downhill and exploded into a million pieces. Staying strong through these times seemed impossible. But pushing through and eventually coming out the other side can make you a better and even stronger person than before. You just have to believe that you can get through anything that is put in front of you and make it happen.

It was the beginning of February, and the snow had melted quite a bit. It was the weekend, so I did not have school, and John and I were hanging out outside. We decided to go back into the apartment, and I heard everyone talking but did not make out much of what had been said. My stuff had already been put in a box because I always kept my things together. I never knew when something might change and I would have to move again. It was a good thing that I did this too because something was about to change. My aunt told John and me to stay inside and sit on the couch. So we did, but we were not sure what was going on. Then we heard a knock on the door. When my aunt opened it, there was a person standing there who I had never seen before. She introduced herself and said that she was from Clermont County Jobs and Family Services. Immediately, my stomach sank, and I knew what was going on. It turns out that my aunt decided that she could not handle taking care of all of us kids anymore so she called Child Protective Services to come to take us away.

When they came to take us away, I assumed it meant all of us kids, but in reality, it was only my brother John and me. Shane was already at my uncle's and Erica at my grandparents. Instead of being put in foster care, the uncle that had taken Bryce before said he could move in with them, and Tracy had gone to live with another family member that I cannot remember. So it turned out that John and I were the only ones left, and no one wanted to step up and keep us out of foster care. They took our stuff to the care, and John and I had to just sit there and wait to leave. I was really hurt, knowing that I was being separated from my siblings even after all the torture they had put me through in the past, but at least I was still with my brother John.

There are many times in life where you will doubt yourself and just want to give up. Getting through these times can seem impossible, but they are not. Fighting to stay alive and overcoming adversity can be as simple as believing in yourself and telling yourself to never give up no matter what.

CHAPTER 10

I had dreamt of the day when I would be free of my family, but when the time came and it was actually happening, I did not want it to happen. It is weird. You hate your living situation, but after living it for so long, that is all you know, and it makes it extremely difficult to accept change. And now we were being forced to uproot again and go live with someone we had never met. At least my siblings had gotten to live with a family who they knew, but we had never even seen these strangers who were going to be taking care of us from then on. I remember being so angry that I just started yelling at my aunt. I just tried to say anything I could to make her feel bad for what she had done. It was not the mature thing to do, but I was upset and had to release some of the anger that had been welling inside of me for so long. The anger that I felt was more about having to make a major change and the fear of not knowing than it was about being taken way from my family.

I did not want the social worker who had come to pick me up to see how I was reacting, so as soon as I saw her, I quickly stopped, but I still wanted to keep screaming at the top of my lungs. There was no way of telling what kind of people we were about to be handed over to, but there was nothing I could do about it.

The drive only took about fifteen minutes; the home we were going to was in Milford, Ohio, where we were already living. It turned out that the neighborhood that we were going to be living in was right next to where my grandparents lived. When we pulled up to the house, the family was waiting for us, and they seemed like nice people. John and I just stayed silent because we did not know how to react. They greeted us and were very kind. It was a nice house, and two of their three kids were living with them, so we got to basically meet the whole family right there. There were four of them there to meet us. Ed and Mary LaFlamm were the parents, and there were Nathan and Ashley, who would now be our foster brother and sister. Ed and Mary had another son, but he lived in North Carolina and was a part of the coast guard.

Someone had helped us take our belongings inside the house and led us to where we would be living. I guess they had known for quite a bit of time that we were going to be coming because they had a room already set up for us. We went up the stairs and into a room with bunk beds. They told us that was our room now. For the first time in my life, I had a bed, but I did not know how to react to it at first. We were silent for a while, just trying to gauge the situation and get used to being there a little bit. Ashley's room was right next to ours and so was the master bedroom. Down in the basement was where Nathan slept. There was his bedroom, a second living space, and a pool table. Ed and Mary welcomed us with open arms, which was a show of generosity and kindness that I had never seen before. They just wanted to make us feel comfortable and did everything they could to do so. The first night being there, they ordered pizza, and it was one of the first times I had dinner with an entire family, and they were trying to make me a part of their family. I admit that I was more than just a little guarded toward their family at first. I did not want to believe that they were good people who just wanted to help. But being with a family I could not trust was all I knew up to this point.

They did not want to push us too much or anything like that; the whole family had been patient to get to know us and to make us feel at home. Over the entire weekend, we had started to feel more and more comfortable with them. They were genuinely good people and truly did care for our well-being. Where we lived was in a different area, and we were supposed to change schools. But the school that we were already attending had made arrangements for a school bus to change its route and pick us up since it was already close to the end of the school year with only a couple of months left. It was nice not having to switch schools after moving homes for once.

We lived in a cul-de-sac, and it had a basketball hoop, so when it was warm outside, we could go out and just enjoy being outside playing basketball. Living there was way different than anything I could have imagined. It was hard to imagine a good life with good people after everything I had been through, but this family that we were with now proved that there really are good people out there that are truly good and care about others.

Every day that we spent staying there, we grew closer and closer to the LaFlamms, and it made it easier to not be in contact with our real family. Even though we were growing closer to them, I can look back now and say that we never fully let ourselves become a part of their family. It is a weird situation to want to leave your own family and then when you do it is hard to completely let go.

As foster children, we had to be assigned caseworkers to come and visit us each week to make sure everything was going okay with our living situation; it is as much to help the foster parents as it is to help the foster child. They would come to the house, and at first, it was like an interrogation, but over time, it became more than that. Instead of just being forced to meet with a caseworker, I began to enjoy the meetings. The first caseworker that I can remember, her name was Andrea. She was very nice, and even though she had to do her job and ask certain questions, I could tell that she began to care about how John and I were. Having so many people around us that just wanted what was best for us was extremely unusual but in a good way.

The one thing I truly did not like about being in foster care was we were forced to go through therapy. I know at first it was to make sure I was coping with being in foster care and everything else that had happened to me, but after a certain amount of time, it just became annoying. Every time that I had to go, it was the same thing over and over again. It was good to be able to have someone to just vent to if needed, but sometimes, all it felt like was more interrogation and just asking the same questions every week.

Because I was in foster care, I had good health insurance and had to get yearly physicals, dentist visits, and eye exams. I think that up to this point in my life, I have only had maybe one dentist visit, at least that I can remember. Plus with all of the chaos of living without water at times and all of the other crazy things that had unfolded, my teeth were not in good shape. On the first dentist visit that I had after entering foster care, I had more than four cavities. Also, I had to get glasses. My eyes were not too bad, but they were starting to get worse and worse, and it became harder to make out what the teacher was writing on the chalkboard, so I was glad to have glasses. The insurance only covered certain glasses at the eye doctor, and the selection of glasses was not very good. The only glasses I could get were the biggest glasses they had. So of course, after getting these and having to wear them to school, I had to face a new round of scrutiny from my classmates.

At home though, I was actually starting to feel like part of the family at the LaFlamms' house, and it was a really good feeling. It was springtime, and it was nice to be able to go outside almost every day. Ed started to teach John and me about sports, and we would toss a baseball around a bit. And since we lived in a cul-de-sac, there were a bunch of kids that were around the same age as John and me. We eventually started to become friends with them, but at first, they did not exactly understand why we were living with Ed and Mary.

Eventually, we were allowed to have visitations with our siblings. We would all meet up at McDonald's and eat together and just be able to talk. This became an every-week thing, so it was nice to see them more and more. Since it was springtime and it was pretty warm out, we started to meet at a local putt-putt place too. It was cool because they also had go-karts there, so we got to have fun racing one another.

Ed had been teaching me a lot about baseball, and I began to love playing sports a lot. Even though their house was not meant to be a permanent home; Mary and Ed treated us as if we were normal kids and offered to sign both John and me up to play sports. We both wanted to play baseball. I never had the chance to do anything like that before, and it was exciting. I started getting really good at it too, and after school was done, it was great to be a part of the sports team. I actually made some really good friends by playing baseball too, which was a new experience for me too. Ed or Mary would always be with us at our practices and just supported us 100 percent.

Eventually, we found out that my mom had been living in Milford, and she had been granted visitation rights to see John and me. I did not know how I felt about getting to see my mom again, but I knew that John really wanted to see her. If my mom had done everything she was supposed to and had a job and stayed clean and sober, then our visits would get more and more frequent. If all went well for her, then we would eventually be allowed to go live with her again. I did not really want this any more than I wanted to see her. But after she had been making her visits and jumping through all of the hoops she was supposed to, I thought she had actually changed. And after a while, we actually were allowed to start staying the night with my mom on the weekends.

I preferred being with Mary and Ed though, but I think John liked being with my mom more. Why would he have thought differently? The only thing my mom ever truly did against him was when she abandoned us. He was so young that I do not know if he understood everything that had happened anyway. Of course, after seeing my mom more and my siblings, we had to talk about it more and more in our therapy sessions.

One thing that I never took for granted ever again after moving to Mary and Ed's was being able to take a shower every day, that and having food every day, three times a day. I cherished the time I spent living here. There was still that fear in me of not knowing if we would be changing homes or even being forced to move back with my family.

Even though things were a lot better while living there, I still had to deal with everything, and being able to play sports was a huge stress reliever. I loved to play baseball and basketball, and it was like, when I was on the baseball field or shooting hoops, nothing else mattered except for me and the game. Ed had taught me a lot, but my coach was the one who really took the lead in teaching me everything I knew about baseball. His name was Steve Myers. One thing he always liked to do was tell stories. He was a great guy, and he always had a lesson to teach the baseball players he was coaching.

During the summer, as foster children, we were not supposed to stay home alone for long periods. Well, I was too young to watch myself anyway. So during the days while

Mary and Ed were at work, John and I had to go to day care. It was actually fun to go. The teachers were great, and we were allowed to play sports and games while there. We did not always have to go to day care though; sometimes Ashley would watch over us. I always looked up to Ashley LaFlamm. She was a great foster sister, and she treated me like I was her real brother.

I had a lot of fun that summer, playing baseball; the only bad thing though was that our baseball team was not very good. We actually lost every single game that summer, but we had a blast just playing baseball. One of the kids on my team lived in Mary and Ed's neighborhood. We became really good friends, and since we lived so close to each other, we would hang out sometimes.

The summer had almost come to an end, and I had to start preparing for school. I was about to start the sixth grade. I guess my mom had been doing everything she was supposed to because, as I had mentioned already, we had been allowed to start staying the night with her on the weekends. We did not know it at the time but she did not live in a very good neighborhood. There were always kids fighting or just causing trouble in general. I really did not like going over to her house on the weekends, but I did not let her know that.

I do not remember why but John and I had a new caseworker. His name was Mike D. We really liked Andrea, so we were not sure if we were going to like Mike, but he turned out to be a really cool guy, and I really enjoyed getting to spend time with him. But it was only once a week, and we also had to go to therapy still.

The school had been in full swing, and I liked going to school still. It was still my way of getting away from life. Now it had been for different reasons; I no longer had to worry about getting food every day or being abused by my family.

It was just nice knowing that school would always be a constant in my life. Even when I did have to switch schools when I was younger, I knew it was something I was good at. I just hoped that that one thing would never change. As before though, I had been picked on a lot in school, but I did not mind it so much. I was quite adept at ignoring bullies.

Every weekend, we would go to my mom's house. We were supposed to be spending time with her and building our relationship back up. But that never happened. Every single weekend that we spent over there, she had her boyfriend over and would spend most of her time with him. I really did not like going over there, and eventually, it was not just because of my mom. As I said before, it was not a good neighborhood. I had made a couple of friends but not many. There were a lot of kids who just liked to start trouble and cause fights for no reason. And since I was one of the smallest kids around, they chose to target me. Big surprise, right? I thought I could deal with everything that they threw at me, but eventually, it was more than words and would become physical. There was a big gathering of kids playing football, and some of my friends were playing, so I joined in. It started off just with everyone having fun until my team started winning. My team had won the game, and one of the kids from the other team started pushing me around, so I just asked him to stop, and I walked away. He did not like that. He wanted me to fight him, but that was not who I was, so I just kept walking away. Then he started to run after me, and I took off, running for my mom's house. He caught up to me at the door and pushed me into a wall. I had no choice but to defend myself. I could not get in the door because he was blocking it. He just started hitting me and pushing me into the wall. It was not like fighting my brother, who was smaller than me and could not cause serious injury. This guy was bigger than me and was not going to stop hitting me until I fought back. I was tired of being pushed around, and I hit him back. What else could I do? I just started swinging as hard as I could, and I was just hoping he would just stop. No matter what I did, he would not stop, then one of the times I swung at him, I do not know what happened, but I felt a bone in my hand just snap, and at first it did not hurt. I could not stop defending myself though. Luckily, he finally stopped. I had successfully defended myself without getting hurt too badly. I went inside and had to put ice on my hand and wrapped it up. I guess the adrenaline had worn off because my hand started to throb with pain.

After being picked up by Mary and Ed, I had to lie to them and tell them that I had just been hurt playing football. I was used to lying about injuries, but I hated having to lie to them. They took me to get my hand checked out as soon as they could, and it was broken, so I had to get a cast put on it for six weeks or so. The worst part about it was that it was my right hand, which is the hand I write with.

Time was going by pretty quickly, and winter had already come; the best part was that I had finally been able to get my cast removed. I had never broken anything before that, so it was a new experience. I was extremely happy to be able to take a shower without putting a bag around my arm for once. It was nice to have the cast taken off, but I had to get used to fully using my hand again. Throwing a baseball and shooting a basketball was difficult with a cast.

I like going outside during the winter now because Mary and Ed had helped us with getting clothes that actually fit, and we have good winter jackets. Behind one of the neighbors' houses, there was a hill, so we got to go sled riding too. Also, in the neighborhood, there was a small pond, so when it was cold enough and the water froze over, we could skate on it. I had never been ice-skating before, so Mary and Ed had bought John and me ice skates to use. It was extremely fun, but it definitely hurt when I fell. And that being the first time doing it, I fell a lot.

Christmas came; it was the first Christmas since being in foster care. I cannot remember if John and I had spent time with our family, but I knew that the most important time was spent with the LaFlamms. They had taken me in and treated me like my parents should. I cared a lot about them, but that is not to say that it was perfect. I was growing up, and their parenting styles were completely different than what I was used to, so eventually we would clash a little, but that made it more like a real family though. At least I was never verbally or physically abused while living with them, and that was the most important thing for me. I never had to live in fear of harm, hunger, or homelessness while staying with them, and for that, I am truly grateful.

Returning to school was not the same as it was before. I still liked going, but I did not have to use it as a means of escape anymore. I finally could find peace at what I now called home. Although I still had to share a room with my little brother, who caused problems at times, I still had a room and a bed to just lie in and be at peace. I was finally beginning to feel happy about my life, so I had to question what was going to happen next. There was still a doubt in my mind about whether or not I was going to have to move again or end up homeless, but it was not dominant, and I could push the doubt to the back of my mind and almost forget about it.

School was going pretty good for the most part, and I had actually joined some extracurricular activities. I still had to deal with being bullied though. After school was done, a couple times there was a group of students who stayed behind, and I was usually the last one in the class because of where my desk was placed. The teacher had left the classroom, and when she did, the students would block the door so I could not leave. At first, I did not think that they were doing it on purpose, but I was quickly proven wrong. One of them looked out to make sure no one was coming while the other two turned to me and started pushing me into a corner. They knocked out what was in my hands to the ground and started hitting me. If it was just one person, I probably could have gotten away, but that was not the case. Their bullying nearly made me miss the bus, but I made it just in time. I never said anything to anyone about it, but it would continue to happen. So I would just have to hurry up and run out the door before I could be cornered again. It did not happen as often, but they would still sometimes trap me. That is when I found out there was an after-school tae kwon do class, so I asked Mary and Ed if I could sign up, and they said yes. It was not like I wanted to learn to beat someone up. I just wanted to be able to defend myself if needed.

My schedule with school and meeting with a therapist and Mike D. became kind of monotonous, and it had already been a year that I had been in foster care. The school year was in full swing, and not just the school. At the end of the school though, there was a meeting to tell the sixth graders about joining sports teams at the junior high school that I would be going to school next year. I did not think about joining anything, but one of my friends convinced me to join cross-country. I did not even know what it was at first, but I joined anyway. Also, since it was time for school to be coming to an end that meant that baseball was going to be starting soon, so I really looked forward to that.

In the neighborhood that we lived in, there was also a pool, so we could go swimming almost any time that we wanted to during the summer. And this pool was a lot nicer than the pool that was at the hotel I had to live in before. Ashley would take John and me swimming all the time, and

I liked getting to spend time with both of them. Most of the time, John and I would get along, and Ashley was like a real sister.

That summer had gone by extremely fast, and before the end, I had to start cross-country practice. I did not know what to expect, but it turned out that I really like it. Cross-country was just long-distance running. At first, it was difficult because I had never had to run long distances before, but I got good at it. I kept getting better and better, and eventually, I started to run for fun. I know it is weird to think of it as fun, but it helped clear my head, and I had become a very competitive person by that time, so I loved to run against other people.

Also, during that summer, Mary and Ed had taken us on vacation, and it would become something that we would do every summer. We never went anywhere crazy like Disney World or anything like that, but we would travel to different states, and generally, we would visit their family. The first vacation that I remember, we went to North Carolina, and they introduced John and me to their other son, Ben. He was in the coast guard, and we had to go out to where he was stationed to meet him. Ben was a great guy, and we instantly got along with him, and it was not hard to think of him as an older brother. Actually, we like him so much, when we went to go get a haircut, John and I both just said we wanted the same haircut as Ben. When we met Ben, we also met his girlfriend, Katie, and she was very nice as well. Katie was also in the coast guard. They lived pretty close to the ocean, so for the first time, I had the chance to see it.

Mary and Ed were happy to let us meet their family; they would actually introduce us as part of their family too. The rest of their family lived in upstate New York and Canada. So they also had taken John and me up there to meet them. Just like Ed and Mary, they welcomed us with open arms. I actually started to look forward to the times when we would vacation to see their other family members. The only bad things about our vacations were the drives. Sitting in a car for ten hours is not the most fun I have ever had, but after arriving at our destinations, it made the trip worth it.

Being put in foster care, being adopted, or being taken in by another family is a big change for anyone. It is hard to fully let yourself become a part of their families even if you are welcomed with open arms. I urge anyone that is put into this situation and is taken in by a family that grows to love you, do not be afraid to start caring for the family and becoming a true member of their family in return. Letting your guard down for anyone can be tough, but it can really pay off in the long run and create a wonderful relationship with a loving friend or family.

CHAPTER 11

School had started back up, and I was now in the seventh grade. I did not know where time was going. Maybe it was because I was happier now than ever, but time was just flying by. I liked being in junior high; I did not have to deal with being bullied as much. But it still happened; mainly it was just verbal abuse though. Somehow, in the sixth grade, someone thought that it was funny to start calling me by the nickname Collier Dog. It was pronounced call-yer-dog. This nickname would end up sticking with me all the way through high school. I do not know why I let it bother me so much, but it really got under my skin. I think that I was finally at the point where I was tired of putting up with any kind of abuse from anyone. After all that I had been through, I finally was standing up for myself.

The seventh grade was a big year for me. I was in school sports, and I joined the choir. I had been in a choir before, but now there was an audition choir, and I actually was able to make quite a few friends this year. I had always been an outcast, but now that was finally beginning to change. One of my friends kind of forced me to audition for the concert choir, which was the audition choir, and I actually made it. I was proud of myself. I never had to try out for anything, and I never expected to try out and actually make it. This made my confidence grow tremendously.

At the start of the year, I had still been visiting my mom on the weekends, but that was soon to change. My mom had tested positive for drugs, so we were no longer allowed to visit her and stay the night. Now our visits had to be monitored by the county and in a room with a camera. I cannot say I was surprised by my mom doing drugs again. I actually kind of knew already. For one, she never followed through with any promise before, so why would she have started now? Also, I knew what marijuana smelled like, so when she had it at her house, it was pretty obvious.

Now that we could not see my mom on the weekends like we had, we were allowed to have visits with our siblings at McDonald's again. John and I really looked forward to these get-togethers. Over time, my mom just stopped showing up to our scheduled visits, and it became evident that she did not care about us at all anymore. The same as before, all she cared about was finding a way to get her next fix, whether it was weed or pills or whatever she was using at the time.

It did not bother me too much that my mom did this, but John was quite upset about it. He thought we really had a chance at getting out of foster care. A couple months later, in April, I turned thirteen years old.

Since my mom had lost her chances at getting custody of me and John, we were put up for adoption. I did not want to be put up for adoption because that would have meant that I would have had to move yet again and maybe change schools. Luckily though, since I was over the age of twelve, I had the legal right to make the decision of whether I wanted to be put up for adoption or if I wanted to just stay as a foster child. I, of course, chose to stay as a foster child and stay with Mary and Ed.

Choosing not to be adopted would have unforeseen consequences. There are certain laws and rules that foster youth have to follow. We foster youth are separated from normal children and are treated differently than we should be. Some of the rules are understandable. But the government should not put rules on all foster youth when not all foster youth are the same. Also, some laws are different from state to state.

One of the first times it became apparent that I was not treated the same as a foster youth was when I wanted to stay the night at one of my friend's house. I was told that I was not allowed to because I was a foster child. There are ways to be allowed, but sometimes getting permissions and the process seemed too long to even attempt. Mary and Ed would break the rules sometimes and let us stay with our friends, but most of the time, it made it easier to just have our friends stay the night at our house. They tried to make us feel like normal kids, but there was only so much that they could get away with. Another issue was with being allowed to stay home by ourselves. We were supposed to have a babysitter, and Ashley would be able to watch us, but when she was out, then we had to be looked after by one of the neighbors.

The neighbor kids would all hang out quite a bit and go to the movies or to an amusement park. John and I would never get invited; they knew that we would probably not be able to go, so they would not even ask. I knew why they did not ask, but it still hurt a lot. We were not supposed to drive with anyone under the age of eighteen without proper permission, and even if we did drive with someone, the county had to have a copy of their driver's license and a copy of their insurance card. Sure, that does not seem too bad, but I did not feel comfortable asking anyone. What was I supposed to say, "Excuse me; Can I have a copy of your driver's license and insurance in case I have to drive with you in the future"? That's not the easiest thing to ask someone. So I just never asked and avoided the problem altogether. It was not Mary and Ed's fault that the rules were like this, but they were the ones that had to enforce them.

After I had turned thirteen, there was only a month and a half of school left, and it went by slowly, but finally, it had come to an end. Another school year was over and I was actually looking forward to summer for once. I knew that I was no longer going to be staying at my mom's on the weekends and that Mary and Ed usually planned a vacation, so there was much to look forward to. It is sad to think that even at that age I did not want to live with my mom again. I remember that my caseworker, Mike, had asked me what I thought about being in foster care. I was only twelve when he asked me this, but I answered him by saying, "I am glad that I was put in foster care. I know that it is what was best for me and my brother." I was very mature for my age, but it was more out of necessity than anything. I had to grow up fast to be able to survive the ten years I lived with my family.

During the days of the summer, John and I both had to go to the extended daycare center, but it really was not too bad. At least on an extended day, there were other kids my age, so I did not only have to hang out with my little brother. One thing that I did not like about summers was that I did not get to stay in contact with too many of my friends from school. I never really liked talking on the phone, and I was not able to just go hang out with them any time I wanted. But summer vacation was not that long, so it was not too bad. I was used to not spending time with friends and really not even having friends, so it was easy to cope with it. I would play basketball every day to help me stay in shape and to try and get better. I had tried out for the junior high basketball team the year before and did not make it, so I wanted to get better in hopes of making the team in the future. One of my favorite things that summer was getting to play baseball again. I played every position except for catcher, but my favorite was shortstop and pitcher. But my coach did not let me pitch very much. Actually, that year, the only game he let me pitch in was the very last game. By the time the baseball season was over, it was already time to start practicing for cross-country. We would practice at the school every morning during the week for hours. So I would have to practice in the morning and then go to an extended day after that. I had greatly improved and was now one of the top runners on the team.

Time did not always fly by, but eventually, the summer did come to an end, and school started back up. That summer, I found out that my dad had been released from prison. I was ambivalent about it though. Sure, I wanted to see my dad again just to see if he was going to change from his old ways, but also, he had done a terrible deed, and it was not something I could just overlook. We had already been told that we were not going to be getting out of foster care ever unless through adoption, so it was not like I expected to go live with my dad. I think John was happier than I was about my dad being released, and I think that he might have believed that my dad would take him out of foster care. But when faced with reality, he could not really handle it. I, on the other hand, had already accepted that this was where we would be living for a long time, and as I said before, I was happy to be in foster care.

That summer while visiting with my siblings at McDonald's, something happened that I did not see coming. Since my mom had lost custody, she decided that it would be a good idea to sneak around and try to see John and me while we were with our siblings. Of course, she did not care about the fact that if she was caught, then we would no longer be allowed to see our siblings anymore either, but when did she really think about others anyway? Sneaking to see us was not the end of her tactics either. After trying to sneak and do this a couple of times, she had one of my sisters ask John and me if we wanted to run away and be taken out of foster care. They wanted us to say we were going for a walk one evening, and they would have a car waiting to pick us up. Their plan was to pick us up and then flee the state to California, where my mom had gone when she abandoned us. Of course, I did not like this idea. I immediately told them no and to stop asking us. I should have told Mary and Ed what they had asked of us, but I hoped to keep seeing my siblings at least a little, and I knew if I told them, then I would no longer have that privilege. But it did not matter anyway. I am not sure why but slowly and slowly my siblings decided to just stop showing up at our visits. Then it was decided that there was no point for us to keep meeting if only one person was going to show up. There were times when we would show up and no one else would come at all, so we would be left sitting there, waiting, to no avail. It became clear that we had been abandoned by everyone in our family now. I understand that sometimes things do come up and people cannot always make it to appointments or scheduled meetings, but at least let us know before not showing up somehow. But that was too much to ask of them; it would not have mattered anyway because eventually, no one showed up at all. Of all of the things that my family had done to hurt me and my brother John, I think this is the one that hurt the most.

I tried not to let it bother me by putting everything I had into school and running. It did not take too long to get over it though. I mean, what else could I have expected from a family that had abused and tortured me for ten years? I wanted to give them the second chance that I believe everyone deserves, but they ruined it and basically spit at my face.

That year, I hoped to be more involved with school and be a normal child or at least try to feel like one. I tried out for the audition choir again and made it in, and I continued to run cross-country. It was going pretty well other than a few minor issues with being bullied still. I did not let that stop me though. I just brushed off the bullying attempts and pushed forward, determined to be a better person. I never understood why people would just start picking on me for no reason whatsoever. But I did not spend too much time thinking about it because my family had no reason to treat me the way they did but it happened anyway. Some people are just cruel sometimes, but like I said, I believe everyone deserves a second chance. So I would forgive those who had caused issues for me and walked all over me.

People might say that I have been too forgiving and that I let others step on me and take advantage of me too much, and they are mostly right. I could never belittle someone or be cruel to another person intentionally because I know how it feels, so if someone asks for my help or for anything, I am too quick in responding yes.

The school year had gone by pretty quickly so far, and I tried out for the basketball team again. I had practiced practically every single day since the tryouts the previous year. I even played in the snow in the middle of winter. I let nothing stop me at becoming better and better, and I tried to become the best. But when tryouts came, even though I felt that I outperformed some of the other players, I did not make the team. The coaches really did not even need to hold the tryouts because they already knew who they were going to pick. I know I may sound like I have a biased opinion, but I do have proof. Before the tryouts, there were two students that were basically guaranteed spots on the team. But before the tryouts, they had both broken their legs in different situations. Even if they did not play half the season and did not even tryout for the team, they made the team. How does that happen? If you cannot tryout for a team, then you are not supposed to be able to be on the team. I do not dislike those two students because I knew who they were, and they were pretty nice kids and were actually pretty good at basketball. I just do not like it when certain kids are singled out and treated more special than others undeservedly.

I continued to focus on school and friends. The only problem was that I could not really hang out with my friends outside of school except for the ones that lived in my neighborhood. The school year literally was flying by, and it was already time for Christmas break before I knew it. This was now going to be my third Christmas with the LaFlamms. I enjoyed spending Christmases with them. I felt that I was finally at home somewhere and that nothing could go wrong. Of course, a little while later, I would find out that I was wrong yet again, but I did not have any clue of the matter at the time.

CHAPTER 12

School had resumed, and I do not know if it was because the days were being so monotonous or what but time just went by in a flash, and before I knew it, it was close to the end of school and finally time for summer again. I was officially done with junior high and was going to be entering high school in just a few short months. Baseball was starting up, and I was excited. One of the teachers from the extended daycare was the freshman baseball coach at the high school, and he agreed to come and watch some of my games that year. He liked to go to the ball fields to see the competition and see what kind of prospects he might have coming to his team. I was the starting pitcher for my team that year, and I was really good. Of course, I was not the only pitcher on the team. There was also my good friend Kevin. That summer was exciting, but since I was old enough to take care of myself, I really did not like having to go to daycare anymore. But I could not stay home by myself with John because I was a foster child.

Even though I had to spend my days at daycare, the summer did go by pretty quickly. Mary and Ed had taken us on another vacation to upstate New York and down to North Carolina to see Ben and Katie again. I like going down there very much because Ben and Katie lived right near a river, and John and I could go tubing downstream and just relax.

After our vacations were over, it was nearly time to return to school. Normally, I would have started practicing with the cross-country team, but I decided not to run this year, which I truly regret not doing to this very day. I cannot really say why I did not decide to run that year, but I wish that I had. I did however join the JROTC program through my school, but that was not a sport, and I joined the choir again. As a freshman, there was no option for the audition choir or concert choir except on rare occasions. But there was a regular choir, which I joined with quite a few of my friends. This year was off to a good start but would prove to be challenging for me. At home, I had my own room since Ashley had moved off to college, and she had been there for a couple of years now. I was not sure if she would eventually move back, so I did not call it my room. But now that it had been a few years, I was happy to say that, for the first time in my life, I had a room all to myself. I was still happy just to have a bed let alone my own room. The added benefit of not having to share a room with John was definitely a plus. I loved my brother, but he could be the most annoying person in the world sometimes. Every single night before going to bed, he would make random noises just to annoy me. I hated it, but I did not have to worry about that anymore.

School was going well, and my grades were looking good. There really was not much of an issue with dealing with bullies or anything like that because all I did was hang out with my friends in the hallway while I was not in class, so I did not have to worry about being bullied much at all. However, that would change later on in the school year.

Everything seemed to be going well at home and at school. I started to condition with the basketball team before the tryouts. It was a good way to stay in shape, and the coaches could see me play before going into the tryouts. I conditioned as much as possible because I was motivated to make the team that year. There was nothing that was going to stop me from making the team. By the time tryouts were closed, I was excited to show how good I was. During the conditioning, the coaches had me competing against some of the upperclassmen, and I proved to be able to keep up pretty well with them. Then, the week of the tryouts, I had come down with a really bad illness. I thought that I might just miss one day and then still be able to make the tryouts, but I was wrong. My health just got worse, and I could not keep anything down. Mary had taken me to the doctor, but they could not say for sure what was wrong with me. I was going to try and go to the tryouts anyway, but I was too weak to do anything. I lost more than ten pounds in just one week. Mary had tried to explain to the coach what happened to see if there was any way for me to try out after I was up on my feet again, but they refused to help me out and said that I had to make it to the current tryouts, and that was the only way. But I could not do that. I was way too sick, so I had to give up on making the team that year. It really hurt because when I returned to school, I talked to some of my friends who had made the team, and they were disappointed that I was unable to make it because they believed I deserved a spot on the team too. It was not the end of the world, but I really wanted this for myself.

I continued with school and forgot about basketball for a little while. Baseball conditioning was starting soon, and that was my true love anyway. Plus the coach had already seen me play the past summer and was giving me good vibes about making the team. The tryouts were not for another couple of months, so all I could was condition and be ready for when the time came.

Winter break had come and gone, and that year, we had gone to visit Ben and Katie over the holidays. It was great because I hated the wintertime, so getting to go south even for only a week was a nice break from the cold weather. It still got a little cold in North Carolina, but it was nowhere near the same as in Ohio. They lived in the middle of the

Smoky Mountains, and the views were amazing. It was a good change of pace from our normal routine at home.

We returned home, and school continued as usual, and it was moving by quickly. I was still conditioning with baseball, and it was getting close to the tryouts. This semester started off not too bad, but I was in a gym class with the kids that had bullied me the most in the past. I thought that maybe, since we were in high school, things might change, but I was wrong. I never did anything to cause any trouble for them other than beating them in sports in gym class, but after every gym class, they would say rude comments or something to me in the locker room. I brushed them off as much as possible, but at some points, I just could not handle it anymore.

Normally, I try not to let the small things bother me, but I could not handle everything that was happening at this time. Someone in the school was trying to start rumors that I was gay, and people would go down the hallways yelling "Jeremy Collier is gay!" I wholeheartedly support those in the LGBTQ community, and I have many friends that are a part of it. But to have people spreading rumors that I was gay really hurt me and bothered me more than it should. With that and being bullied after gym class, I just could not handle it anymore.

Baseball tryouts had finally come, and I was more ready than ever. I did not want to let anything bother me that day so that I could just focus on doing my best in the tryouts. Most of the day was going well, and I was getting nervous. Gym class came, and I tried to avoid the other kids as much as possible to avoid any issues that might throw me off my game. After the class was over, one of my friends in the class was talking to the kids I had issues with, and he made some comment that I agreed with, so I said, "Yeah, you're right." That was when one of the bullies just told me to shut my mouth. I did not know what his problem was; I mean, I was agreeing with something that he was saying. I thought that it was over, but when we entered the locker room, things got worse. They were trying anything they could to start a fight with me, but I did not want to fight. Then they started pushing me, and I thought I was going to explode. But I did not; there were six of them and only one of me, so I knew if I defended myself, it would only make things worse. We left the class and were waiting for the bell to ring so we could go to our next class, but their comments did not stop. So I stayed behind to try and get away from them, but I was already at my breaking point. I was so angry, but I could not think clearly. I just wanted this to stop, but I was not about to get into a fight. I regret my next actions more than anything in my life. I walked around a corner, thinking there were lockers there, and just swung my fist at the wall. Unfortunately, there were no lockers there, and I just hit straight concrete. I felt my hand snap and immediately knew I broke my hand. How could I have let them get me so angry? I had been through worse bullying than that before. I walked past them and showed them what I did, and they immediately shut up, and I walked myself to the nurse. My hand did not hurt that much, but I was so angry with myself for what I just did that I started crying. I knew that I had just blown my chance to tryout for baseball. After what happened, the coach told me that I was going to be his starting pitcher, and that made me feel even worse.

I did not want to think about the opportunity that I just lost, but the cast on my hand was a reminder of it every day for the next six weeks or so. I still had to go to gym class every day and see those kids who pushed me over the edge, but after what had happened, they did not bother me anymore. I am not happy with what I did, but there is no changing it now, and I had to live with the consequences. Even after all that I had been through I had let a bully get to me. No one is perfect, and even with tough skin, I was pushed too far. But I could do nothing about it anymore, and I had to look to the future and learn from the mistake I made.

The rest of the school year went pretty smoothly, and I did not let anyone bother me after that. Being in gym class with the kids who decided to bully me was not fun, but it was not all bad. I met some people who I would eventually become really great friends with.

The school year was over finally, and summer was starting. I had at last been able to get my cast taken off. Just having had my cast taken off, Mary and Ed wanted me to be cautious, but I immediately wanted to throw a baseball. The day I had my cast removed, I actually had a baseball game, and my coach wanted me to pitch. I was excited, but Mary and Ed were a little worried that it might be too soon, but they let me make the decision in the end, and I chose to pitch. I was happy to be back playing baseball. Whenever I stepped on the mound, everything around me just melted away, and it felt like I was where I was supposed to be. After throwing a little, I felt comfortable with my hand. The only problem was that I could not throw as fast as I used to. I was disappointed with that, but I was still grateful to be playing again.

That summer went by in a flash, and when I returned to school, I was happy to see my friends again. Everyone was bragging about being able to get their temps and being so close to being able to drive, but I could not share in their excitement. As a foster child where I lived, I was not allowed to have a temps or a driver's license. It was the one thing that gave a teenager a little bit of freedom and made them feel like an adult, and I could not experience it with my friends nor was I able to drive with them. So when they did get their license, they started to hang out more outside of school, but I was never included because they knew I would not be allowed. That year was probably going to end up being more difficult than the last one.

Near the end of my freshman year, I auditioned for the concert choir and made it. I enjoyed singing almost as much as I enjoyed playing baseball. There, in concert choir, I ended up meeting one of my best friends, Justin Ray. He is a great guy and would always try to help keep me smiling. He knew the situation I was in and was very supportive. Having friends to lean on and give you support can be more influential than you think. Something as little as making you smile every day can really brighten up your day and give you a more positive outlook on life. Also, that year I was put in an English class with one other person that would have one of the biggest impacts on my life. She would become my best friend in the whole wide world, and I would not be where I am at today if it was not for her. Her name is Ashley Allen. But at the time, I did not know how important she would end up being to me.

That year was crazy and would prove to be hard to handle. The school part was easy, but there was a very big change happening, and there was nothing I could do to stop it. Ed had been working at a paper company for a long time. This job required him to travel at least two weeks out of every month, it seemed like. Sometimes he was even gone for six-week trips. At his company, he knew that there were going to be layoffs coming soon. He did not feel like he might lose his job, but he was ready to stop having to travel so much, so he chose to leave and saved someone else a job. He and Mary had to make a hard choice, but they felt that it was best. However, Ed had found another job, but it was nowhere close to where we were living then. In fact, it was over fourteen hours away. They were going to be moving near the coast of North Carolina. So what was going to happen to John and me? We did not want to have to deal with moving again and changing schools. I had finally felt at home, and now this was happening. Mary and Ed cared a lot about us, and they showed it by what they did next. They still moved, but they had asked us to go with them.

We were just foster children; they could not just take us with them. So they had asked us to become their children, not just foster children. They wanted to adopt us.

I was the older child, so this decision was on my shoulders, but I had to make the decision for both John and myself. The decision was hard because not only would we be changing schools and towns but we would be moving fourteen hours away. I knew that John had still hoped to have a relationship with our biological family and would hate me if I chose to go with Mary and Ed. But on the other hand, I knew it would be best if we did go with them. Even though it was what was best, I admit that I was being a little selfish. I did not want to leave Ohio. I did not want to have to start over completely once again. I had finally started to feel normal and have friends and relationships. There was no way that I could just start over again and forget all of my friends. It was a hard choice to make, but I finally decided what to do. Even though there was no guarantee we would be living in Milford still when we changed homes, I still wanted to take my chances. We were not going to be moving with Mary and Ed. I could not pull myself to tell them what I had decided; it felt wrong. They kept asking me, and I just said I was still thinking about it. Eventually, though, they sat John and me down, and there was no choice but to give them the answer. It was hard to break the news to them.

I did not want them to feel that we did not care about them, but how else could they have felt? Even though they were upset, they still cared about us and only wanted what was best for us. Winter break had come, and I never thought that that was going to be the last Christmas that I would spend with them. They still bought us Christmas presents and treated us like we were their children, but it was hard to face what was soon to come. After Christmas, we had all gone on a trip with the church we were attending.

But when we came home, it was, unfortunately, time to start packing.

Unfortunately, there were no foster homes in Milford to take us, and we were going to be forced to change schools again. It was a big chance that we had to take, and we had lost. We had begun packing when we had gotten home from the trip when we received a phone call. It turned out that someone had come forward in Milford and wanted to become foster parents so that John and I did not have to move. It was John's basketball coach. I had never met the guy, but I was thinking that he must have been a great guy for making such a huge decision and become a foster parent just for John and me. I knew it was going to be a new home and a change in my life. But I also knew that I had friends around me to support me when I needed them and to help brighten my days if I needed them to. It is always important to have positive influences around you in life. It can keep you from making bad decisions, and they can help you in the times when you make those decisions anyways. That is why not being afraid to trust others is so important. Having a support system can help you see the light at the end of the tunnel and get you through rough patches in life. High school is not the easiest time for anyone. There will always be challenges, and having good friends or family can really put the odds in your favor.

CHAPTER 13

We had been excited about the news, but we had to start saying our goodbyes also. It was hard to say bye to Mary and Ed, but it had to be done. John's birthday was on January 7, and we moved into his coach's house on January 8. Of all of the homes I have ever lived in, I definitely preferred living with Mary and Ed over all of them. They were legitimately good people, but that does not mean that it was always perfect. I admit that sometimes, I almost hated having to deal with all the rules, but I never hated them. Now that I look back on everything, all they wanted was what was best for us, and John and I were better off because of everything that they had taught us. But while living there, sometimes it felt like everything was a lesson. When we first moved in, we were not the most well-mannered kids. How were we supposed to know proper manners when we were only cussed at and abused? One of the things that I disliked most was how they wanted to teach us manners. It is one thing to have to say please and thank you; it is a pretty understandable thing to ask for. But when it came to teaching us table manners, I did not like what we had to do; it was more annoying than anything. The biggest issue was with putting our arms on the table while we were eating. Every time that we had messed up, no matter where we were at, we had to go outside and count to the number Mary told us to count to. I understand that she wanted us to know good table manners, but it was not fun to have to go outside and count while we were out at a restaurant. One form of punishment that my brother John really was not fond of was writing lines. If we got in trouble for certain things, we would have to write lines. John had to write them a lot. They were strict at times about what we watched and what kind of music we listened to also. They were religious people, which was not a bad thing because they helped me find the Lord. But they did not like us watching any movie that was not PG without passing it by them even after turning fourteen and fifteen years old. So I would just tell them that I was going to one of the neighboring kids' house to watch a Disney movie and just end up watching something else. I did not listen too much, so it was not hard to not listen to anything that they would not approve of. Plus there was a lot of music that I did like that was Christian music, so I would not have to lie about listening to it anyway. One thing in particular that bothered me was that they did not allow more than one hour of TV, computer, or video game usage per day, not individually but altogether, and I really liked to watch certain shows that were an hour long each, and at the time, we did not have anything like DVR or something to record them on. It was not the worst thing, but playing outside for hours on end can get a little boring at times, and I would just want to lie down and relax and just watch TV sometimes, but I could not. The good thing that came from this though was that I was in really good shape, and my sports abilities improved all the time. I never had to worry about being abused physically, verbally, emotionally, or in any way, but having to deal with the changes in parenting styles was a bit hard sometimes, especially as I was getting older.

I was now in my second of what would become three foster homes. Our new foster parents' names were Steve and Amanda, and they had two sons, Jake and Aaron. Their house was a bit smaller than Mary and Ed's, and I was back to sharing a room with John again. At first, I did not mind. I was just happy to not be leaving Milford. I had not even mentioned that I was supposed to be moving to most of my friends. I did not bring it up until after I was told I was actually going to be able to stay in Milford.

At first, it was great living there, but it was just for a short time. John had already known Steve a little bit and was friends with Jake, so it was easier for him to get used to living there. It was different for me. I never connected with Steve or Amanda, and it ended up being a not-so-good living situation for me. The first couple of months were fine. They had actually lived right next to a couple of my friends, like Ashley Allen, so I had expected things to get better with time. They, unfortunately, did not. I had done everything I could to try and make it a good living situation. I had talked about what was happening with my current caseworker, Karla; she had been with me since I was at Mary and Ed's. She was one of my favorite caseworkers that I had ever had. Not that I did not like my other caseworkers, but she had been on my case through the roughest times and for a longer period than any of the other caseworkers that I had been assigned to.

Like I said, I did everything I could to try and make it a good living situation, but nothing I did would ever help. John was always starting arguments with me and just bothered me in any way that he could. Jake started to do the same thing. I tried to get along with Jake by doing all of his chores for him, but it did not matter. Even if he did not do them, it was not like he would get into trouble. Steve and Amanda had decided that they had to choose between spoiling their children and punishing their children when they did wrong. They chose to spoil them. Steve said that there was no median between the two, so they decided to spoil Jake and Aaron. Jake knew he could get away with whatever he wanted and would purposely do things to prove it. Since I was not their real child, they had no problem with punishing me and grounding me for things that I did not even do. Jake would start a fight or something, and I would be the one to get into trouble.

It was like I was living with my real family again, and I wanted out. There was one difference though, and that was that Steve and Amanda never hit me. The only escape that I had was school and when I spent time with Karla, but I only met with Karla once a week, so that was not much of an escape. My sixteenth birthday had come and gone, and unlike all my friends, getting my driver's license was not an option. They could drive and get away from home if they had issues, but not me. I had to be stuck at home and get yelled at by Steve and Amanda over something stupid all the time. I never did anything to even get into trouble, which made it worse for me. I would understand if I was a bad kid and I was smoking or sneaking out and drinking, but that was not the case. All I did was go to school, come home, do everyone's chores to be nice, and then I would do my homework and keep to myself. Even though they showed a great disliking for me, Steve and Amanda loved John. They would actually kid around with him and show love for him. They were nothing like Mary and Ed.

Mary and Ed would show how much they cared for us, but Steve and Amanda never expressed any kind of emotion like that for us or for each other, for that matter. During my stay there for exactly eleven months, I never once saw them hug each other or even say that they loved each other. Even though they did not show too much love toward us or each other, it was easy to tell that they preferred John over me and wished that they did not have to take both of us in. Steve always gave John attention and would make jokes with him and play around with him, but I did not want to connect with him, and he did not want to connect with me. I would have gladly just left or gone to a different home, but I was afraid of leaving my brother John. I did not know if he could handle having not me with him anymore. Eventually, it would not matter either way.

As time went on, it became more and more evident that they did not care how their son, Jake, treated me. He probably could have gotten away with murder with them. Jake would start an argument or do anything he could to cause an issue, but I would be the one who would get into trouble. No matter what I did, there was no way of convincing them that their son was the one that started it. I, of course, had a lot of pent-up anger and would snap at my brother John for the small things sometimes, and we would just bicker like normal brothers sometimes too. If John and I argued just a little, they would act like I was trying to kill him and blow the whole situation out of proportion. More than once they called my youth pastor from church to come and talk to me like I needed to be exorcised or something. When the summer came, I was all alone and had no way of venting other than to Karla, but once a week was not enough. Eventually, Steve and Amanda had put me into anger management because John and I were arguing like normal brothers. But they told the counselor that I was out of control and made me out to be the bad guy. I could not talk to this counselor because all he wanted to do was "fix" my anger issues. Steve would come into the sessions, and that just made it worse.

During the days, we were no longer going to extended daycare anymore, and instead, we had to go to Amanda's workplace, which was also a daycare. But at Amanda's workplace, all we could do was sit on our hands and do nothing. This was literally one of the worst summers of my life. Amanda would yell at me for just lying around because I was setting a bad example for the kids. What else could I do? I did not work for the daycare, and it was not like I was going to have fun playing on a swing set. Eventually, I was allowed to go back to extended day and be a volunteer teacher. I was allowed to assist the first and second graders. This made my days go a lot faster; I really liked having an impact on the kids' lives. The children I was looking after looked up to me, and instead of just having to lie around, I was able to interact with the kids and play games. I was able to teach them things like dodgeball. Extended day was not just a daycare for the younger kids; it was almost like a school too. The teachers would help teach them how to read better and help them grow. But when I had to go home, the life was just sucked out of me, and I was put into a very depressed state of mind.

I could not rely on just going to extended day to help resolve the issues I had at Steve and Amanda's house. The summer was only a couple of months long, and it was almost over. They ended up taking us on a vacation at one point, but I did not look forward to it at all. We ended up going to Hilton Head; it was a beautiful place, but there was not much to do other than go to the beach and enjoy free time. I could not relax though. John and Jake hung out, and I chose to stay by myself. I just wanted a way out, but it did not look like it would ever happen. I was finally at a point where life was looking up when I was living with Mary and Ed, but like all the good things in my life so far, it did not last. I found myself longing to be back in school again and to be away from everyone at home. I just wanted to be able to see my friends again and to be able to smile. Looking forward to this did help and kept my spirits up a bit. I found myself having to keep hoping for things to get better, and I knew that they would. Summer was not forever, so it was just a task of waiting at that moment.

The entire vacation in Hilton Head was very lonesome. I could not stand to be around Jake and John, and I did not want to ruin the vacation for John. I would just walk down to the beach alone or just go to the condo's front office, where there was a public computer to use. There was really only one good part of the whole vacation. I went to the beach by myself and was just walking around and watched some people fish. They were catching small sharks in the same area where some others were swimming. Then I looked up, and about fifteen feet out from the shore, there were three or four dolphins swimming by. It did not make the whole trip amazing, but for that short amount of time, I could not help but appreciate nature and have just a glimpse of hope for the future. Getting to see dolphins swim so close by was really a spectacle, and it was something I could think about to keep my mind busy.

There was nothing else that helped this so-called vacation go by faster, and when it was over, I thought I would feel better, but at least there, I was able to walk around alone and get away from everyone. At home, there was nowhere to go. I could not just take a walk and hope to escape the prison I was in. The only thing I was looking forward to then was to return to school and use that as a way of forgetting what was supposed to be a life. I did not have to wait long because our vacation was toward the end of the summer.

School was a sight for sore eyes for me. I was able to see my friends and was happy for a break from home. Some of my teachers had already known about my situation and were very supportive, which made the school year a lot better. Junior year in high school is probably the hardest one to deal with and is probably the most amount of work, so having all of that support was really helpful.

Another thing that really helped me was that now that I was already sixteen, there was an independent-living kind of class for foster youth every Monday night to help teach us basic life skills. They helped with teaching us how to budget our money, find apartments, and job search. I really like going to this class, and my caseworker, Karla, was one of the teachers, so I was able to spend more time with her and away from Steve and Amanda. Karla would pick me up and drive me to and from the meetings because she did not live too far from where I lived. One of the perks of these meetings was that we received money for showing up. It was only ten dollars, but it was a nice bonus. Five dollars was for a few homeworks, and the other five was for showing up. I always made sure I received the whole ten dollars. I tried to save up as much money as I possibly could. The other teacher's name was Katie; she was a great teacher, and I enjoyed going to these classes with her and Karla. I was the only guy in the class; that made it a little uncomfortable, but I dealt with it. All of the other foster youth smoked cigarettes, so they would go outside and smoke when we had a break. I just stayed inside and talked to Katie or Karla. I used this time to help deal with whatever problems I was having and to just build friendships with both Katie and Karla. They were really supportive of me; if I had not had these moments to spend with both of them, I do not know how I would have survived living at Steve and Amanda's. Normally, I would never have issues with anyone and could build friendships with almost anyone, but that was never going to happen with Steve or Amanda. I tried to keep my head up about the entire situation, but after a while of being talked down to and treated like a second-class person, I almost started to believe that I really was a bad person and everything that had ever happened to me was my fault and no one else's.

Having supportive friends and my time with Karla and Katie helped me get through these times, and I knew that it was not my fault. I had done nothing wrong to be treated the way I had been treated my entire life. So I had to just keep my head up and know that I would not have to live there forever. I was glad to be able to see my friends like my friend Justin; he always was able to make me smile, which helped me not think about having to return home after school. Jake did not make it easy to keep my cool though;

he liked to purposely try to set me off. One of the biggest examples was shortly after school started. In my English class, we had to write papers quite a bit even though they did not have to be too long. So of course, I would need to be on the computer to type my papers. Well, I guess the computer was technically Jake's, but that was the computer that Steve and Amanda told me that I could use and that Jake would share it with me since he never really used it that much. After a couple of times using it, Jake started putting a password on the computer so that I could not get on. He would refuse to let me on it at all. Steve and Amanda did not care because Jake was their little angel who could do no wrong. Well, I figured out his password and used the computer anyway because I needed to do my schoolwork. Once Jake found out that I cracked his password, he flipped. He decided to change the password again, but this time, he left me a note on the computer. It read, "Ha-ha, Jeremy, try and get on the computer now. You are never getting on this computer again. You're just a stupid foster child and an SOB!" I was so enraged I went off. I wanted to just hit him, but I knew that would do nothing but get the cops called on me or something. Even after showing Steve and Amanda the note he wrote me, they did not care. All they said was "Well, it is his computer, and he can do whatever he wants." I hated them for this. All I wanted to do was do my homework, and this was what turned out of it. I was trapped with nowhere to go with a family that hated me, and I truly despised them.

Now that I was sixteen, I wanted to get a job for two reasons: one was to make money, and the other was to help me get out of the house. But since I was not allowed to have a license, Steve and Amanda had to be the ones to take me to and from work. I think that they wanted to be away from me too, so they were willing to take me whenever I had work. I did not like my job, but it beats being at home. Going to school five days a week and working helped time go by faster. The months were going pretty quick. It was already near the end of November, and I received some news that made things even worse. Steve and Amanda had sat me down and announced that they were basically going to be kicking me out. They did not want to "deal with me" anymore, but they wanted to keep John. So now, there was no choice in the matter, and John and I were splitting up. I did not mind because I knew I could handle it, but I did not know if John could. He was fourteen years old, but he was not as strong emotionally as I was.

Not only was I being kicked out of this foster home and being separated from my brother but I was going to have to change schools and would probably never see any of my friends again. I was not sure how to react. I knew that my new foster parents were going to be nice people because I had met them before. But I did not want to move in with them and change schools. Unfortunately, I had no say in the matter.

I went to school the next day and had to break the news to some of my friends. I did not even tell some of my friends because I was too heartbroken. I was going to be in my third foster home within one year. I did not want to even think about what else could go wrong.

The days were just dragging by, and I was very depressed, and it was almost time to pack up my things and tell my brother good-bye. I was talking to my friend Kevin, and he said he told his parents about what was going on, but what could they possibly do to help me? I packed all of my things and was counting the days until I was going to be officially kicked out of Steve and Amanda's house, and then Steve said he needed to talk to me. I was not sure what was going to happen. Were they going to just tell me to leave now, or was someone on their way to get me? I had no way of telling what was happening. Steve said that I did not have to change schools after all. I thought maybe he wanted to play a cruel joke on me before I left or something like that. But then he told me that they found out that a family had come forward and were going to become foster parents so that I could stay in Milford. It was my friend Kevin's parents, Will and Karen. I guess there really was a way that Kevin's parents could help. I already knew both Will and Karen because Will was one of my baseball coaches, and Karen used to work with my first foster mom, Mary. I cannot express how overly joyful I was to hear this news. I called to talk to Karen to thank her and see when I would be able to move in. She said that I could come over whenever I felt comfortable. I, of course, wanted to get out of there as soon as possible. I had to say good-bye to my little brother, and the next day, I was moving into Karen and Will's house. I always had fun when talking to Will at baseball practice, and he was a really funny guy, so I thought that living with him and Karen was going to be great. Plus, Kevin and I were already really good friends, so now we were going to be like brothers. I had moved into Steve and Amanda's on January 8 and moved out on December 8 of the same year. Like I said, it was exactly eleven months.

CHAPTER 14

I was happy to be living with Will and Karen but had to get used to living with Kevin and his sister, Brittney, and I still had to go to anger management but not for long. After going to my first or second session after moving in with Will, the counselor said that I seemed a lot happier now that I was not living with Steve and Amanda, and she could tell that their home must have been the issue. So she signed off to release me from anger management, and for one of the first times since being in foster care, I no longer had to go to counseling, and it felt great.

Karla was still my caseworker, which I really was happy about. I had changed too many caseworkers already, and I really liked spending time during our meetings. We would just go to Wendy's and eat and talk. Most of the time, we did not even have to talk about foster-care issues anymore.

I had moved so close to Christmas, and I was not sure how it was going to be. I made sure that I went and bought Karen a small gift to show my appreciation for what they did for me. To my surprise, they bought me a couple of presents, and I could not have been happier at that point. I thought that this was going to be the perfect place to live and that nothing could go wrong. Before the Christmas break started and I had moved in with Karen and Will, I was still in school, so I was able to tell everyone that I was moving in with Kevin and that I no longer had to move away. A lot of them did not even know that I was supposed to be moving away, so I explained why I did not tell them, and they mostly understood but still wished I had said something.

That winter break had gone by faster than most, and I could not believe it had only been a year since I had left Mary and Ed's house. It felt like a lifetime. I tried to make sure that I stayed in contact with Mary and Ed for at least a little bit so that they knew what was going on. I actually still stay in contact with them to this day.

School was different since I had moved again. It was a like a weight had been lifted off my chest. I was really happy for once. Kevin was able to drive, so he would drive Brittney and me to school every day. My teachers were made aware of what happened and were still very supportive, but I did not need the support as much at that time. I was a lot happier then. I was still working, so I had to be taken to work all the time and picked up, which I have always hated. I do not like having to rely on others to get me from place to place, but at the time, I had no choice. Not being able to drive really set back a lot of the plans I had for my junior and senior years. As a junior in high school, I had enough credits that I could have graduated a year early, but I knew that I was unable to drive until I was eighteen, so there was no point. I was angered by this, but there was nothing I could do. Being able to graduate high school early and then start college a year early could have changed my life dramatically, but there was no way of me getting to college without being able to drive. Also, the next year, my senior year, since I did not graduate early, I could have done what was called postsecondary schooling, which was where I could have started taking college courses while still in high school, but just as before I decided to not even think about it as an option. I would have had no way of getting to and from the college classes without being able to get my license.

Not too long after living with Kevin, I notice a change in him. He was not the same friend that had asked his parents to take me in. I thought I had known him, but I was wrong. On our way to school every day, both he and Brittney would smoke multiple cigarettes. I could not breathe because of it. Plus I had to show up to school smelling like smoke. I just figured it was just a small issue to deal with, but I never knew that things were just going to get worse and worse.

At the beginning of February, I started being really good friends with Ashley Allen again, and we were talking all the time. So I decided to ask her to be my girlfriend, and she said yes. It just so happened that the day I asked her out was the six-year anniversary of me being put into foster care. Ashley was one of my biggest supporters during the rough times, but for a short time, we did not speak much, but I was really happy to be with her now.

Spring was finally here, and I was glad to start throwing a baseball with Kevin as the temperature was getting warmer and warmer outside. The honeymoon phase of living there was over, unfortunately. I was always doing chores while Kevin and Brittney did nothing. It was like they were too good to clean. But I put up with it because they had helped me stay in Milford. Little by little, it just kept getting worse and worse. I was still working, but I had to switch jobs because I was not getting enough hours. I liked to work, but I did not want to be the only one in the house doing chores and helping out. I was allowed to hang out with Ashley a little bit on the weekends, but for some reason, Karen did not like it too much, so she started making sure I had more chores to do, so I complied. Kevin was able to drive, so he was allowed to just leave whenever he wanted and did not have to worry about anything, but I was stuck at home, doing whatever Karen and Will wanted. Once it was warm enough out, Will and Karen wanted to plant some trees around the house and told me I had to help them out, so I did, assuming that once Kevin came home that he was going to be helping out. Not too long after starting, Kevin did come home, but he was not even asked to help. I was sitting there, digging away and working hard. All he did was come home and take a shower, and then he just said, "I am leaving to see my girlfriend." So Karen just said, "All right, we will see you later." But when I asked if I was allowed to go see Ashley, it was a big N-O! It was completely unfair, but there was nothing that I could do since I could not drive. Things like this kept happening more and more often, and I started feeling more like a servant and less like a part of their family.

Actually, one time, Will's family had a get-together, and I came along so that they could introduce me to everyone. I was just hanging out after meeting everyone, and one of Kevin's cousins came up to me and said, "You are not a part of our family, and you never will be. You are just a foster kid." I was taken aback by the sheer rudeness of this comment. I never expected his cousin to say something like that to me. So I just sat there and did not even give him the gratification of a response. More and more it was being made sure that I was nothing more than a foster child and second-class citizen in their eyes.

I had resented living there, and it had only been six months or so. My seventeenth birthday had come and gone, but it did not matter. As time went on, I found out more and more about Kevin and Brittney, and it was not the best of things. Kevin was basically an alcoholic and a compulsive liar. You could not believe anything that he said. If he was out late, he made up some unbelievable story to tell his parents, and of course, they would buy it. He had a bunch of empty beer bottles and cans in his room and would get drunk on the weekends either when his parents were gone or just when they went to sleep. Brittney was only fifteen, but she was always drinking too, but that probably was not even the worst of it. I found out that Kevin used to be a huge pot smoker and that Brittney still was. I do not have any respect for people who choose to take part in such behaviors, especially after having to deal with how bad into drugs my parents were. Being seventeen did give me some happiness with looking towards turning eighteen and finally having a sense of freedom, but I had to wait another year before that.

One of the biggest issues with Brittney was that she like to hit me a lot. Every single day, she would just start punching me and punching me for no reason at all. Even if her parents saw it, they would not do anything. I should not have to go to my room and shut the door just to avoid more abuse. Everything just kept reminding me of living with my parents, and I hated that. They were supposed to be a loving and supportive family, and they were at first. But now, I resented them and wished I lived somewhere else. Karen and Will were both pretty heavy drinkers also. When they drank, they were not like my parents, but every single night, Karen would pass out on the couch with a glass of wine in her hand. The only thing I was glad about was that I did not have to deal with them screaming and yelling or hitting me when they were drunk, like what my parents would do. It was a good change, and at that point, I did have to be happy for the small things like being able to stay in Milford and having Ashley in my life. I did not like being around all the drinking, but it was tolerable since I was not being physically abused during those times.

I would try and hang out with Ashley as much as possible and just get out of the house, but that was not always possible. Her parents were very nice, and her mom started treating me like her own son, and that really helped me out.

I still met with Karla every week, but I did not tell her about how bad it was living there. I did not want to have to deal with moving when I was close to being a senior in high school. So I just kept my mouth shut and acted like everything was fine.

Even when there was no reason for it, Kevin would call off work quite frequently. He kept telling his boss that he was in the hospital because someone was dying or that his sister was going into labor. None of which were actually true. Eventually, he just quit his job, but he had gotten a new one. I was actually sick one day, so I had called off work, but I told Karen that my employer told me I did not have to come in. She called my work and asked them why they were letting me off work. Once she found out that I called off, she went off on me. Kevin did not have to worry about anything like this because Karen did not need to know his schedule since he was allowed to drive himself. But since she was my transportation and was being nosy about every little detail of my life, she had to know everything. Just for calling off one day of work, she decided that I had to be grounded for a whole month. It was the end of the school year, so I was grounded for the entire first month of the summer. They took everything away from me; I could not watch TV, get on the computer, talk on the phone, or see Ashley. It was a severe punishment that was undeserved. I never did anything wrong, yet I was always getting the worst punishments out of anyone. I kept working and just sat in my room alone for the entire month. I never complained once about my grounding because I knew it would only make it worse. I hated not being able to see Ashley since seeing her was the only time that I was happy anymore, but I was not allowed to talk to her or see her. I could sneak and talk to her on the phone at work when I got off each night though. But five minutes a couple of times a week really was not great.

When I was finally ungrounded, the first thing I wanted to do was go see Ashley, but I was not allowed to do so immediately. Karen had to sit me down to make sure that I knew why I was punished, and they made it out to be like I was a criminal getting parole who had to make sure I was not going to commit a crime again. They told me that they were going to unground me a lot sooner but that I just kept complaining. This was total crap. I did not complain once. I never even mentioned my grounding at all, but I think that Brittney and Kevin told them that I did to make sure I was in trouble longer. They loved to make other people's lives miserable. I was finally able to start seeing Ashley again, and it was like a breath of fresh air. Her mom was so nice to me, and I felt more at home the few hours I was with them than when I was at Karen and Will's house.

During that summer, we all had to go to Will's friend's house, which was right along the Ohio River. I thought it might have been nice to go, but it was not what I expected. It was extremely boring; all I could do was sit around and do nothing. All of the adults were drinking all night, and Will and Karen were letting Kevin and Brittney get drunk and do whatever they wanted. They all were trying to push me to drink, but I refused every attempt. I do not drink beer or alcohol at all. My parents were drunks, and I would not take part in one of the things that caused my life to be a living hell with them. That is all that anyone did all weekend long—drinking and more drinking. They did go out on the river in a boat, but of course, they made sure they had plenty of beer with them.

The little "vacation" could not end soon enough. I had talked to Ashley a little bit over the weekend but not enough. I really did not want to be with Karen and them that weekend, but I had no choice. I was happy to see the end of the weekend and be able to get away from so many people drinking. Will and Karen worked during the day, so I would try and see Ashley if I could, but most of the time, all I could do was stay at the house while Kevin left to see his girlfriend. Brittney did not leave that much; she had people over all of the time though, and they were always guys. She was only fifteen years old, and she was having a different guy over every other day, and let's just say that she was not a virgin. There was no way that her parents did not know what she was doing, but I could not tell if they were just ignoring it or if they truly did not care that their daughter was sleeping with a different guy at least every week. I never thought to say anything because I was afraid that I would get into trouble for something stupid. Life was already bad enough there, and I was not going to be the one to make it worse.

A little later that summer, we had planned on returning to the river again, and I was not happy. I was talking to Ashley about it, and her parents offered to let me stay at their house for the weekend while Karen and the family went down. I talked to Karen about it, but she immediately said no. I think that she liked to see me in pain watching everyone drink while I just sat there disgusted by their actions. There was nothing I could do; there was no other way to deal with the situation than to just let it be.

The same things happened as last time except things were a bit crazier. Kevin was really drunk, and I basically had to babysit him because he almost killed himself. During one of his drunken escapades, he decided to run toward the river, which was about a twenty-foot drop from the bank. He ran straight for it and almost went over the edge before I was able to catch up to him and tackle him to the ground. I had to pick him up and throw him over my shoulder and force him into a tent to make sure he did not try that kind of stunt again. Brittney, on the other hand, was drinking with a bunch of young guys in a tent and having "fun" with each of them. This was not how I wanted to spend my weekend. I was the only sober person around, and there was no way out.

Finally, we were able to go home and return to just sitting around. Kevin and Brittney still would get drunk when Will and Karen would go out of town for the weekend, but at least then I could just go to my room and watch TV or try and go see Ashley somehow. Was this really how my life was supposed to unfold, babysitting a bunch of drunken teenagers as they abuse me and treat me like a servant?

At last, the school year had come to an end. That summer was awful; the only thing that I liked was being able to see my girlfriend. I also had quit my job; Kevin helped me get a job working with him. I liked it a lot more than my last job, and I made more money, so I was able to save a lot more too. Since we worked together, we were able to drive to work together sometimes, so I did not have to wait until Karen was home all the time too.

I was happy to be back in school though; I was finally a senior in high school. My relationships with Karen and Will were almost nonexistent, and I was okay with that. Karen was not supportive of me at all, and she made that evident. Ashley's house was on the way to school, so I made Kevin drop me off near her house, and I would just drive with her in the mornings. I hated driving with Kevin and Brittney in the morning. They smoked, and it was making me sick. I was always sitting in the back, so all the smoke blew right back into my face. Kevin was able to get out of school an hour or so earlier than Brittney and I because he did not have a class during the last period of the day, so we would have to wait for him to pick us up, so I would try and ride with Ashley when I could and hang out with her after school.

Spending time with Ashley was the only thing I wanted to do every day. Going home with Kevin and Brittney and having to deal with Karen was a horrible feeling, but I kept telling myself that I would be in college the next year, and then I would not have to worry about it. It was early in my senior year, so I made sure that I applied to the college I wanted to go to. It was still pretty early, so I only applied to my first choice to start, and that was all I needed. I was accepted to Wilmington College. I was really excited when I received my acceptance letter, but Karen did not think I should be. She said, "It does not matter that you were accepted, Jeremy. You are not going to amount to anything anyway. You are just a foster kid, Jeremy. You are just going to be another statistic on a wall. You're probably going to end up in jail and homeless." Wow was all I could think; did she really just say something like that to me? I could not believe it; that proved that she did not care about me whatsoever. I was just another foster child, just another statistic on a wall—one of the most hurtful things anyone has ever said to me. The words just bounced around in my head until they hurt. I never did anything wrong to these people, but that was how they felt about me. If it were not for my girlfriend and her family, I could not have made it through living there with Karen and Will.

It is hard to be happy with what you have rather than be angry about what you do not. But learning to appreciate the small things can really give you a better perspective. Over time I have had to realize this over and over again, and every time it has become more and more evident. Being happy for the small things can help you see that some of your problems sometimes are not a big deal. Focusing on the bad things can make you overanalyze the parts of life you do not like and can bring your mood down. Simply taking a deep breath and just thinking about what you have to be thankful for can help broaden your mind and can change your whole outlook on life.

CHAPTER 15

A month or so later, I was just hanging around in my room, trying to avoid contact with anyone in the house, and I started having excruciating pains in my abdomen. I did not think anything of it at first, but the pain persisted, and I could not handle it. I went down to Karen and told her something was wrong and explained how I was feeling. All she said was that I should take some aspirin and go lie down. I was in so much pain; lying down did not help. There was no way of telling how bad this could have been.

The next day, I was feeling better, but my stomach was still hurting a bit. I went to school as usual and just went about my normal routine. On the days that I did not have work, I tried to hang out with Ashley as much as possible, at least whenever Karen had granted me permission. I loved spending time with her, but around this time, we had to take her brother to football practice all the time and sit in her car and watch.

This year was already not turning out to be what I had expected it to be. I had known quite a few people who had been gotten pregnant already this year. I love kids, but I knew I would not want to have one in high school. Ashley and I were both strong Christians, so we both agreed early on in our relationship that we were definitely waiting until marriage to have sex. It is just not worth the risk to have a child before we are able to handle it. We had bright futures in college and life to look forward to, and we did not want to make a dumb decision that could possibly ruin that.

School was going good, and I was at least enjoying that part of my life, getting to spend what little time I could with friends during classes and lunch. I was still seeing Ashley after school though, which was nice. One day though, I was eating lunch and my stomach started to hurt really badly, but I thought it was just a stomachache. I continued with my classes, hoping that it would stop hurting soon. It did not; as the day went on, it just got worse and worse. I still went to Ashley's house after school because I did not get to see her too often. That night, we had to take her brother to football practice again. I was not even supposed to be driving with Ashley because the county never had a copy of her driver's license and insurance, which is required since I was a foster child, but I did not care. Ashley and I were just sitting in her car, watching the practice, and my stomach would just not stop hurting, and it was getting even worse than when Karen just told me to take some aspirin and go lie down. I do not cry too often, but my stomach was hurting so bad that I could not help it. After her brother was done with practice, we all went back to her house, and I tried to lie down, but it hurt to move. It was getting so bad that I could not even stand up straight. Then I had to rush to the bathroom because I was going to throw up. I could not stop vomiting; it was uncontrollable. I probably should have been taken to the hospital in an ambulance, but we just called Karen to come and get me. When she finally showed up, I could barely move, and it was hard to make it to the car. She was planning on just taking me home and making me lie down again like that was going to help. Ashley's mom was like "No, you need to take him to the emergency room right now. There is something seriously wrong." She just said okay, and we drove off. I had to hold a trash bag because I was still vomiting profusely. She did not take me straight to the hospital though. She took me to urgent care, which is not really for urgencies. I barely made it through the front doors, and the people at the desk asked what we were there for. They immediately told us that we were in the wrong place. They said that we need to go straight to the ER. Karen should have listened to Ashley's mom, but she did not. After what seemed like a lifetime, we finally made it to the hospital, and a nurse pulled a wheelchair up to the door. They asked me to get out of the car and into the wheelchair but, I could not move. I was in so much pain; I just had to tell them to drag me out of the car, so they did. I was truly scared and did not know what was going on or what was wrong with me.

If I had come in an ambulance, I would have been taken straight back to a room, but no, I had to sit in the lobby, crying from the pain and vomiting into a bowl for everyone to see. I was getting delirious due to the pain. I could not even see straight, and the room was spinning around me. At last, I was taken to a room and put into a bed. They gave me some morphine for the pain, but it did not help. I was so thirsty, but they would not allow me to have any water because it could affect certain tests that they were going to run. I wanted Ashley to be there, but she was not able. It was just Will and Karen. They had run all the tests they could and came back. I was waiting for hours in pain, and I just wanted it to end.

The doctors came in and said they were going to go ahead and just check on my appendix and see if that was the problem. I had to be prepped for surgery. Will called Ashley to let her know what was going on and told her that he would let her know what happened. It was well into the night already, but Will called her for me anyway. They came to get me for surgery, and I was scared. I felt like I was dying. Just after being put in the operating room, they hooked me up to gas, and then the next thing I remember, I was being woken up after what must have been hours later. The nurse went and retrieved the doctor and let him know that I was awake. The doctor asked how I was feeling, and thank the Lord, I was feeling better, but I was not sure if it was just the drugs in my system. The doctor told me that they had gone in and were going to go ahead and remove my appendix, but it was already ruptured, so they had to remove what was there. I now had to spend the next four or five days in the hospital. I still could not walk without any help. After coming out of surgery, Will did not call Ashley because it was extremely late, but little did he know that she was still awake and waited for him to call. Since he did not call, she started to assume the worst. Finally, early the next morning, I was able to call her and let her know that I was all right but would be spending a few days in the hospital, recuperating. Other than the reason I was in the hospital, I was glad I was there. I did not have to deal with Karen and them every day. The worse part though was the hospital food. Luckily, Will was nice enough to sneak me some fast food. There was a flat-screen TV in my room with a DVD player, so Ashley brought me some movies to help me get through the next few days. Every time she would visit me, I would try and start walking more and more. The doctors said it was a good idea, but I had to drag my IV stand with me, so I used it as a cane. I was happy to be released from the hospital, but I was not happy to be going home to Karen, Kevin, and Brittney. Will was really helpful at the hospital and offered to stay with me for a couple of nights, so he gained a little more of my respect. I was still unable to walk very well right after leaving the hospital, but Karen did not care. Since I was staying home from school for another couple of days, she told me I had to clean the entire house. I could hardly walk around on my own let alone clean a house. This further supported the fact that I was just a servant to her, someone to do her kids' chores and clean the house for her. I could not protest it though. The doctors had prescribed me some pain medication, which did help, but Karen only let me take it the first day I was home, then she put them away because she said I was going to become addicted to them. I am positive that she said that only because I was a foster child and for no other reason. But there was nothing I could do but be happy that I was alive after such a scary encounter.

Fortunately, Ashley was willing to come over and help me after I told her how Karen said to make sure the house was cleaned and that I cannot take any pain medication. The doctors advised me to not overdo it and to take it easy for a while, but Karen did not listen or seem to care what the doctors said. I returned to school the next week, and it was hard to make it from class to class. I was advised not to lift anything over a few pounds for the next six weeks or so. My girlfriend was gracious enough to help me get between classes. I was unable to do the same job I had at work because it required a lot of lifting, so after returning, I would have to switch positions. Halfway through the first day back at school, I nearly passed out. My teacher saw me, and she helped Ashley get me to the nurse. They called Karen, and she had someone come and pick me up. For the rest of the week, the nurse advised that I only do half days in school until I was back on my feet. Luckily, Karen listened for once and had her mom pick me up from school in the middle of each day. If Ashley's mom did not nearly force Karen to take me to the hospital, I probably could have died because of my appendix rupturing. If it was up to Karen, then I would have just gone home and lay in bed, and who knows what would have happened.

Finally, after another week or so, I was able to move around freely without lifting anything heavy at least. I was finally back into the swing of things and could concentrate on catching up with school. It was a pretty traumatic experience, and I was happy to be alive. Karen never let me have any more pain pills after the first day, so I had to deal with the pain. After school though, I heard Kevin and Brittney talking about how they were allowed to take them recreationally and that Karen and Will had given some of the pain pills to one of the neighbors. I really did feel like I was living with my real family again, and I hated it. There were drunks and now pill poppers.

I had to catch up a lot in school, but my teachers were very understanding about the whole situation. I had to go to the dentist though and had to schedule a time to get my wisdom teeth pulled—another surgery. I was not looking forward to it. There was only about another month or so until Christmas vacation, and that was when I was scheduled to have my wisdom teeth removed. When the time came to have that done, I was not a happy camper, but it had to be done. After the surgery, I felt horrible, and my face swelled up like a balloon. I guess my wisdom teeth were a little worse off than originally expected, and that was why my face was as swollen as it was. The top two were connected to my nasal cavity, so after they were removed, the doctors had to sew the holes shut. And the bottom two were almost touching nerves, so if there was a slip, then I could have lost feeling in that part of my face.

After leaving the hospital where they removed my wisdom teeth, they never gave me anything to help soak up the blood that was still coming from where my teeth were. All of the blood just kept going down my throat, and I could not stop vomiting. That plus still recovering a bit from my appendix rupturing was not the best combination, and I was in a lot of pain. The doctor prescribed some medicine for the pain; luckily, Will was the one that was taking care of me this time and actually allowed me to have something for the pain. But just like before, Karen took them away after a day or two, never to be seen by me again. I knew that Kevin and Brittney were getting into them though. They were not very good at keeping quiet about it or they just liked to brag about it within earshot.

My girlfriend had invited me to her family's Christmas party after I had my wisdom teeth removed, so of course, I did not want anyone to see my face the way it was. I had already met her entire family, and they were extremely nice and fun to be around. I was instantly treated like a member of the family. But that did not mean that I wanted them to see me with my face five times the size it should be. However, I did want to get away from everyone at home, so I agreed to go, and I had a great time. It was a nice event, and Ashley's grandma had given me a card and a little bit of money as if I was her grandson. She always made me feel more like a family member and not just her granddaughter's boyfriend.

Christmas break came to an end, and it was exciting to think that I was in the last half of my senior year in high school. I was proving Karen wrong a little more every day as I was getting closer and closer to graduation. My eighteenth birthday was only three months away, and I could not wait. I knew that I was finally going to be able to get my license. I had been preparing for graduation already and could not wait. Other than having to deal with my living situation, time was flying by. This helped me keep my head up and stay strong while coping with everything.

Kevin had been causing a lot of drama in the house because Karen had told him to stop seeing his girlfriend due to the fact that she was causing issues for everyone in the house and Kevin himself. He never stopped talking to her, and it ended up getting me into trouble with Karen again.

As a senior in high school, to be allowed to walk during graduation, we had to do twenty hours of community service. Kevin and I chose to do ours at the League for Animal Welfare. Literally, all we had to do all day was play with cats and dogs. It was the most fun community service/volunteer work there was. Kevin hated it because it was like he thought he was too good to do it or that he had more important things to do. Every time that he and I would go together, he would only want to stay for like thirty minutes. Since I could not drive, I had to go with him. I knew that he was not supposed to be talking to his girlfriend, but I did not want to get in the middle of him and Karen. She already hated me enough. Before we left the shelter one day, he asked to use my cell phone to call his mom because his phone was dead, so I allowed him to use it. I thought there was something unusual about who he was talking to because he refused to use the phone in front of me, but I did not say anything. Kevin took me home and just dropped me off. I was allowed to go over to Ashley's house that day, so she came over to pick me up. I was talking to Ashley about Kevin lying to me, and Karen was listening to every word I was saying because she was very nosy. She asked me what I was talking about, but I told her nothing, and she kept asking me and then forced me to tell her what I was talking to Ashley about, so I felt that I had no choice but to tell her. She thanked me for telling her, and then Ashley and I left. I knew there was something up because she was hardly ever nice to me, so why now? Kevin was talking to his girlfriend still, which is why he used my phone to call her. After what I told Karen, she went off on Kevin, and for once, he was getting in trouble and I was not, at least that's what I thought. The next day, Karen pulled me aside and started yelling at me again, saying it was my entire fault that her son was getting into trouble. If it were not for me, then she would have never found out that he was talking to his girlfriend still. She was the one that had forced me to tell her, and now I was getting yelled at for telling the truth. What was wrong with this picture?

I found out why Kevin was still talking to her, and it was not good. Karen was so worried about me and treated me like a second-class citizen that she did not make sure her own children were staying out of trouble. But what can you expect from a parent that lets her kids get drunk on vacations and do whatever they want? If she had paid more attention to what her kids were doing and worried less about the one person in the house staying out of trouble, then she might have realized what was going on. Brittney was still having boys over all the time while her parents were out, and then it turned out that Kevin had gotten his girlfriend pregnant near the beginning of the school year. Yet I was the troublemaker in the household. I was not a smoker or a drinker, and I chose to wait until marriage to have sex, but I guess that just was not good enough for Karen and Will. I chose to keep my mouth shut about Kevin's and Brittney's endeavors and issues because I was not going to be the one to break that news to them, especially after getting in trouble for telling the truth the last time.

I continued looking forward to graduation and turning eighteen, but living there was making it hard to stay focused and keep my head up. But the support from Ashley and her family and my caseworker, Karla, made the situation a little easier to handle. Finally, my birthday came, and I was excited, but I did not go get my license yet. A week after though, Ashley's dad allowed me to stay the night, and after talking to him, Karen agreed to let me stay over at Ashley's. I just wanted a break from everything, and that was why I was willing to actually ask Karen if I was allowed, and to my surprise, she said yes. I stayed over on a Friday night, and for the first time in a long time, I had true relaxation, and it was like all of my problems were lifted because I knew that, at least for one night, I would not have to deal with Karen or anyone else at her house.

The next day, I had to wait around for Karen to pick me up, and Ashley's dad had offered to just let me stay the rest of the day and eat dinner with them, so I called Karen and asked if I could. She just said no, no considering it or anything; I could tell that it was not going to be a good day after going home that day. Once she picked me up, I gathered my things and said goodbye to everyone, and thanked Ashley's parents for allowing me to stay over. Once we drove away, Karen started being really mean to me, and she asked me why I was so ungrateful because I had asked to stay at Ashley's for dinner. All I did was ask to stay for dinner, and that was exactly what I said to Karen. But she would not have that. She was yelling something and grabbed my arm and told me to look at her. Then she said, "You know what you are? You are nothing but a selfish and disrespectful bastard." I had enough and was not going to stand for the abuse or disrespect anymore, so I grabbed my things and started walking back to Ashley's house. We were still on her street, so she and her family were able to see me walking. Karen put the car in reverse and backed up to me and yelled for me to get into the car. I told her I was not going to take that from her or anyone else, for that matter, and I got back into the car. She was still yelling at me, but I just ignored her. I pulled out my phone and was trying to call my grandfather, but Karen grabbed my hand and tried to rip the phone out of my hands, so I just gave her the phone. When we got back to the house, I started packing my things, and I was planning on leaving as soon as possible. I called my grandfather, and he said I could move in with him, but my dad and his girlfriend were living there already. I was okay with that. I had to get out of there and was willing to see if my dad had changed at all; anywhere had to have been better than staying there and dealing with the abuse from Karen and her family.

I had to meet with Karla and Karen together that week, and Karen said I was still able to stay there, but I had to change dramatically. That felt like a joke as I was not the one that was causing all the issues. I told them I was not going to stay there any longer because I was not the problem, they were. I was done with foster care and was finally going to be emancipating the system. I was going to miss meeting with Karla though, but she had told me that I was her last client because she was changing jobs. So, either way, I was not going to be meeting with her any longer. That night, I had finished packing what I could, and Karen dropped me off with all my things at my grandfather's house.

CHAPTER 16

Things were finally looking up, but I had a lot of built up anger toward Karen and them. I still had to deal with Kevin and Brittney though because we all worked at the same place now. I did my best to just ignore them, but Kevin was not making that easy. Every time that I was not around, he would start talking about me and my girlfriend behind my back. There was no escaping his troublemaking there. I had thought about telling Will and Karen about Brittney's endeavors with all of the guys she had over and that Kevin had gotten his girlfriend pregnant. But I figured that it would cause more harm than good, and it was no longer my problem to deal with their family.

I looked forward to living with my grandpa, but I never knew how much trouble would be coming in the near future. At first, everything was great. I was getting my temps and eventually my license so I would be able to drive. I had to be picked up every morning by my girlfriend though because I still had a month of school left before graduating. Before I left, Karen made it apparent that I was just going to end up dropping out and become a loser of society. But I knew that was not going to happen. I was too strong for that and would never give up. After everything that she had put me through and all of the disrespect that I had to put up with, I would never let someone treat me like that again. I knew that because of my experience, one day, I was going to fight for the rights of foster youth everywhere to make sure that they are treated like normal children and do not have to go through what I had to.

One of the biggest problems with living with my grandpa was my dad and his girlfriend. They smoked a lot, and so did my grandpa. Literally, when you walked into the house, there was a cloud of smoke that consumed everything, and I had to sleep in that because I was sleeping on the couch or the floor of the living room every night. It was only a small two-bedroom apartment, and there were four of us. But I was willing to put up with the small issues since I needed a place to live in for the next three and a half months before I moved to college. Little did I know that these next three months were going to almost be as bad as living at Karen's house.

The first month was not too bad because I had been able to get my driver's license, and my old legal guardian, Byron, was able to help me get a car, so now I had the freedom that I had always dreamt about. Finally, graduation had come, and I had proved Karen wrong. I had planned on having the best summer of my life, but that was not going to happen. I found out early on that my dad and his girlfriend had a very bad drinking problem and were frequent drug users. They were both on disability and social security, so even though neither one of them had a job, they still had quite a bit of money coming in each month. It seemed like every other night they were going out and getting drunk, and I would end up having to go pick one of them up from some random spot because they were completely wasted. And every time that they got their check, they would end up missing for two days or so without telling anyone where they were going. But it was easy to figure out where they had been going. Even after they returned, you could tell by their demeanor and attitudes that they were still high off one drug or another.

This was a regular routine for them, and I could not handle it, but I had nowhere else to go until I went to college in a couple more months. In what seemed like every night now, my dad and his girlfriend would start fighting, and it made it impossible to sleep while they were screaming at the top of their lungs at each other. During the day, I would spend all my time with Ashley because I knew I would not have to deal with any of those issues when I was with her. Her dad would let me stay over on the weekends, and that made dealing with my dad again easier. But I would eventually have to go home and deal with my dad and his girlfriend. The worst part of smoking was that I could not breathe with the amount of smoke in the house. All my clothes smelled like smoke every day because there was no way of escaping the cloud of smoke that encompassed the entire apartment. At night, I had to sleep directly in front of a fan and right next to a sliding glass door to try and get fresh air so I could try and sleep, but even that did not work.

Kevin was still causing problems at work for me, and then I had to deal with my dad and his girlfriend all the time now. Needless to say, I was not very happy except for when I was spending time with Ashley. I could not wait to leave for college; Ashley did not like it as much though. I was only going to be about an hour away, but with both of us going to college and working, we would only get to see each other on the weekends.

My dad and his girlfriend would get into the worst fights ever; they would literally start hitting each other and threw objects at each other in the middle of the night. Of course, I was the one that had to break it up. One of the times though, I was woken up by someone yelling, but I could only hear my dad. I reluctantly went in to see what the heck was happening. When I opened their door, my dad was sitting on top of his girlfriend with his hands around her throat, trying to kill her. I was not going to stand for this, so I went over and pulled him off, and threw him through the doorway. Still yelling, he and his girlfriend started going after each other, so I had to threaten to call the cops. How could they live like this? If you are going to fight so much, then just leave each other. It was getting closer to the time that I had to leave for college, and I was counting down the days. The fights between my dad and his girlfriend were becoming more and more frequent, and I was done dealing with it, so I went off one day, telling them to stop doing drugs and causing problems for everyone around them. My dad's girlfriend got up in my face and started pushing me and cussing at me, so I gently pushed her away to avoid being pushed again. She acted like I hit her as hard as I could and fell to the ground. My dad jumped forward and threw me up against the wall by my throat, choking me and threatening to kill me if I did anything like that again. I could have easily fought my dad and won, but I was not going to be the one causing trouble, so I grabbed my things and left. I ended up having to start sleeping in my car after that until it was time for me to go to college. This time it was different. I had a pillow and a blanket, but it was still my parents' fault that I was now homeless yet again. My girlfriend supported me, and I was able to stay with her during the day, but I was too embarrassed to ask for help from her parents and just waited until I was able to move into my dorm room.

Finally, the day came, and Ashley helped take all of my things to college with me, and I was finally going to be free. I was so excited and could not wait to start classes; I had finally made it to college and was not going to let anything stop me from achieving my dreams. I remember that the first night I was there, I hooked up my computer and found Karen's e-mail. I had to send her an email to rub it in her face that I made it to college and that I was not going to be just another statistic on a wall like she said I was going to be. She had the nerve to e-mail me back and say, "Congratulations, I knew you would make it. I just said those mean things to you to motivate you to do better." Yeah, like I was going to believe that. I am sorry, but I had never given her any reason to believe that I was just going to give up and not go to college. Now Kevin, on the other hand, did not even do half of his homework in high school, so if someone was not going to make it to college, it was him, not me.

I had to get a different job since I was an hour away from where I worked before. I started off as a teaching major and loved all of my classes. One of my favorite teachers was Mrs. Hendricks. She would let me come to her office, and we would just talk about any issues that I had with my family or school or anything. She became like a counselor to me while I attended that college. It was hard only being able to see Ashley on the weekends, but we knew that we were not too far away and that we were investing into our futures by going to college. Even though this college was my first choice, I wanted to go to college closer to Ashley, but I knew that I needed to have on-campus housing. The closest college that had that was the University of Cincinnati, but I did not want to live downtown near the college; the only stories that I ever heard about living on campus were never good ones. That and I think I just wanted to get away from my family as much as possible—those two things are the reasons I stuck with going to school an hour away. My family kept bothering me while up at college, but most of the time, I did not let it bother me. I just focused on my schoolwork and worked all the time. The year was going by really quickly, and I was excited to be looking toward the summer. The only issue was that the next summer, I had no clue where I was going to be living. I did not want to have to go back and live with my dad and his girlfriend because no good could come from that. I had made plans to stay living on campus during the summer, but I was going to have to work for the school.

The year had gone by so rapidly and summer was quickly approaching. I was nearly done with my first year of college; it was amazing how fast time could fly when there was not as much stress to deal with. Unfortunately, I found out that a great deal of my financial aid had been cut for the next school year, and I had to make a huge decision. I had to transfer schools because I was not going to be able to afford the tuition plus room and board at the college I was currently attending. It was a private college, so the cost of tuition, even though it was in state, was nearly three times the cost of the University of Cincinnati. Because of this I, unfortunately, had to choose to move back in with my dad and transfer to the UC. One big change that occurred already during my first year was that I had switched from an education major to a business major. Business was already my second choice, so I was okay with switching majors.

I hated having to move back in with my dad, but I had no choice. I had nowhere else to go. After the exams, I said my goodbyes to my friends and had to inform them that I would not be seeing them the next year. Ashley had come up with her parents' truck to help me pack everything up and head home. I put my stuff in a storage locker because I knew that my dad and his girlfriend would try and steal anything that they could make money off of to pay for more drugs. It was a good feeling to be a fourth of the way done with college, but having to move back in with my dad put a damper on my mood. After returning home, I was able to get my old job back, which helped because I made a lot more money than the job I was at while away at college. Unfortunately, Kevin was still working there, and I did not know how things were going to progress after that. I did not confront him or anything because there was no reason to purposely start an argument. Surprisingly enough, he came over to me and apologized for everything that he ever said that was mean to me and how he treated me while I was living there. It takes a lot of courage to apologize to someone and admit that you were wrong, so I forgave him. I was ready to forgive him, but I would never forget everything that happened. Like what I have said before, I am all for second chances, but there are some things that I will just never forgive or forget. After that, Kevin and I started becoming friends almost, at least at work. I was still not ready to be friends with him like we were before and was not sure if I would ever want to be friends with him anymore. But I know it is not good to hold on to grudges, and I kept an open mind moving forward. Holding onto so much anger can make you take it out on others and even cause health issues without you realizing it.

CHAPTER 17

Even though I was living with my dad and them, I was still spending my weekends with Ashley and her family. They were my real family now and treated me as such. Over the past year, I had created relationships with my other family members as well. I even started talking to my mom again. I still try to talk to them even today, but I do not want full relationships with all of them unless they stay clean and sober. Unfortunately, at the time, and even now, that was too much to ask for some of them. I gave my mom chances to change again. I did not want her to be my mom, but I did want her to have the chance to be in my life again. She did not take this second chance seriously and neither did any of my siblings except my little brother John. Everyone except John was now using drugs and alcohol, and I did not want any part of that.

My brother Shane seemed to get clean, so I did start building a better relationship with him.

Living with my dad was exactly the same as when I had left, and it was obvious that neither he nor his girlfriend would ever change. I wanted to leave and get my own place or something, but I did not have the money to do so. I did not make enough money while working while away at college, so I had to use credit cards to pay for things at some points. But now that I was making more money, I was trying to save up as much money as possible. It was hard to deal with my dad's and his girlfriend's behavior anymore though, and I was not about to go through the same ordeal as the last time. I do not take disrespect very lightly and was not about to take it from a cracked-out drunk that I had the pleasure of calling Dad. I put my foot down and told them that their behaviors had to change and that they were not going to try and take money from me to pay for their drug habits anymore. They told me to get out of their house and to never come back, and I was more than willing to do so. I was now living in my car yet again. Luckily enough, my girlfriend had told her parents about everything that had been going on without me knowing. The next time I went over to her house, her parents said that they needed to talk to me. I was kind of scared, to tell you the truth because I did not know what to expect. Then her dad asked me if I would like to move in with them. I did not know what to say. I, of course, said yes and could not thank them enough. He knew that I was in college and was trying to do the right thing, plus I had now known them for years, so he knew the kind of person I was. I now had a stable place to live in for once with loving people that would never treat me poorly. Ashley's family had already started calling me a member of the family, but now, it was like moving in made it official. I will never be able to thank Ashley and her family enough for the support that they have given me over the years. After moving in with them, I knew that I would be able to make it through anything, and now, I had support from a great family that only wanted to see me succeed in life.

I had been living with them ever since that day, and it had been nearly three years at that point. They supported me unconditionally and never asked for anything in return. Although there were some ups and downs like in every family, I know that at the end of the day, we supported one another and could overcome any obstacle.

Up to this point Ashley had been through some tough times with me and never wavered in staying by side and helping me get through it. For a long time, I had known I wanted to spend the rest of my life with her but we were still in college and weren't ready to get married yet. However, as our Senior year was nearly over and graduation was on the horizon it was time to officially ask her to marry me. While I was already a part of the family, I still went through the traditional routine of Ashley her father for permission. He made me ask her mom and her brother for permission too just to draw things out in answering. Of course, they all said yes and so I went on to plan my proposal.

Throughout my entire time of being with her up to this point, her family had a weekly tradition of sorts of getting Chinese food every single Friday. I was a bit more of a reserved person in those days and with going to college and working we enjoyed spending time together just watching a movie at home. My plan was simple, I found a website to make custom fortune cookies and had them just put "say yes". We had a day to ourselves and ordered some Chinese from our favorite restaurant and stayed in to relax just the two of us. After eating I made sure I switched out the fortune cookies for the ones I had made. Even when a person knows the answer to a marriage proposal, it doesn't make it any less stressful. You want everything to be perfect and that's not always possible. I remember I had to keep pushing Ashley to open her fortune cookie and she kept putting it off. Finally, she opened it and wasn't sure what to think of a fortune of "say yes", until she turned and I was down on one knee. It was not the flashiest and over-the-top proposal but it was still what I would consider perfect. It was exactly what I wanted, just a moment with the two of us together and enjoying each other's company. She must not have thought I would be able to surprise her when proposing as her first reaction was, "Are you serious? You totally got me!". Pure happiness spread across her face and tears of joy ensued as she said yes.

After getting engaged the rest of the year went by in a blue. And Because of Ashley, I made it all the way through college and to graduation. If not for her and her family, it would have been a lot tougher to get through it all. I graduated college on June 9, 2012, with a bachelor's degree in business administration with a major in finance. Because of Ashley and her family, I have proven time and time again that I am not just another statistic as Karen expected me to become.

CHAPTER 18

Transitioning into life after college can be a tricky thing, especially after growing up in foster care. Looking to start a career and become my own person become an everyday goal I had to work at. Despite all of the bad memories and ups and downs with my biological father I still stayed in contact with him while I lived with Ashley's family. Although he wasn't a great person, he was still my dad and I felt obligated to stay in touch with him and try to have a relationship.

Twelve days after I graduated, I received a call from my grandpa saying that my dad had passed away. He and his wife had gone out the night before and were doing a heavy amount of drugs and he died from an overdose. His wife overdosed as well and was taken to the hospital. I didn't know how to feel when hearing the news. I rushed over to my grandpa's house to be with him and to talk to the police as they tried to put together what happened. Seeing the coroner's office take my father out of the house in a body bag was a hard thing to see. I could not pull myself to watch it, I remember standing in one place and turning my back on them until they were gone. After this, I had to be the one to call all of my siblings and let them know what had happened. This is not a call anyone can ever prepare you for.

I do not know if I was just numb or did not fully process what was going on. But it took a couple of weeks for me to feel any real emotions about my dad being gone. I knew he wasn't a good person had been a drug addict. But I didn't want for him to be gone. Knowing the type of person he was, made it a confusing time for me. I was trying to find a job after graduation while also working through my dad's death and not fully knowing how to feel about it. Coming to terms with it, I had to make myself realize that it was okay to be confused. My dad was never a real father to me, and yet he was still my dad. I think a lot of people find it hard to understand how miss someone who wasn't a good person. After someone is gone, sometimes you start to think about the good things and the good memories, so you start to miss them. But when they are someone with a troubled past, you also have the memories of all of their bad decisions. Just know that this is completely normal to feel this confusion and whirlwind of emotions. You have to let yourself feel each of the emotions to work through them. While it is hard to admit at times, it has been 8 years since my father passed and I still go through some of these emotions and the confusion around missing him.

Although I was still working through my father's passing, I was excited about graduating college and starting my career. Ashley was already working at a nursing home and after graduation, she became a Registered Nurse there. For me, it took about a month, but I had finally found a job at a local company and was ready to put my degree to work and start building my future. To help us out, Ashley's parents let us continue to live with them while we worked to save up money and buy a house. Life after college for me was a big deal for me. It meant a lot for me to be able to find a way to fully support myself and have something of my own.

While having the opportunity to stay with Ashley's parents for a while was what I needed at the time, I was ready to get out and have a place to live with just Ashley and myself. After about a year of working, we knew it was time to move out. It took some time to find a place we liked but we finally were able to find a house. Although we were both working full time, I was not making a ton of money myself, so we had to find a home that met certain criteria for not needing the standard 20% down payment for a home. Despite being good with our money and saving what we could, we most certainly did not have $20-$30,000 to put down on a home. Luckily, we were able to find a way to make it all work out and were able to put in an offer on a home. Growing up and even going through high school life skills classes and college, they do not teach you about the home-buying process, applying for a loan, getting utilities in your name, and many other things that come with being a homeowner. Needless to say, we had a lot to learn in a short amount of time.

When closing day came on the house I couldn't be more excited. I may not have shown it on the outside, but I was overwhelmed with emotion. Living in so many different houses through the years I was never fully comfortable with calling a place home. I knew that eventually I was going to have to move or was going to be kicked out because that was the way it had always been. But now, buying a home with my fiancé, I had stability and peace of mind. The first night of staying there was one of the most comforting nights rest of my life. I had a sense of belonging and safety that I didn't expect. Having a home was something that I always wanted, and now for it to be with my future wife was even better. For the first time, my future felt like it truly was in my own hands and I was in control. There were going to be ups and downs in the future but having a place to call home with someone you love makes it easier to embrace them. Life will always have its challenges, some of which you can never prepare for. Having somewhere to make you feel safe and at home is a greater privilege and blessing than most people realize. It is easy to want a bigger house or a nicer car, and I still find myself thinking that way. But for me, at this moment I was able to look back at where I had come from and see all that I had and all that I had been able to do for myself.

Dreaming of a better future and having goals to obtain the things we need and even the things we want; is something we should always be working on. Yet, taking a step back every now and then to count our blessings and understand what we have today is an important step in our journeys forward. Fear of failing to meet our goals and never getting something that we want out of life can be scary and hard to handle. But reminding ourselves how far we have come and what we have will make it easier to take the risks as you will know that you have something to fall back on.

CHAPTER 19

Shortly after we moved into our home, we were able to officially set a date for our wedding. At this point, we had already been engaged for a year, and since we had to pay for the wedding on our own, we had to set the date for another year out. Planning a wedding is already a stressful time, but not making a lot of money and paying for it ourselves added to it for me. I wasn't going to let this stop us though. Ashley had done so much for me and I wanted to make sure that she had the best wedding that we could afford.

I don't know if it was growing up without a lot, I was a very frugal person and hated spending money if I didn't have to. Ashley was the same way, she enjoyed couponing and shopping at thrift stores for clothing and other items which made it a little easier to start saving money. With some of the planning we knew we had to find alternative options for things like catering and the cake to save money as well. Not having any family to invite to the wedding myself outside of Mary and Ed and their family, the wedding was going to primarily be Ashley's family in attendance so we didn't have to plan for a huge event with hundreds of people. It was just going to be a smaller celebration with around 50 people, which in my mind was a perfect size.

The year leading up to the wedding went by in a flash. As we were getting closer and closer, we had to get the final things in place. Although we spent some money on some flowers, since Ashley is a very crafty person, she helped make a lot of decorations like the centerpieces and my corsage. A local park had an outdoor event space where we could hold the ceremony for a low cast and there was an indoor event space right next to it so it was all in one place. We started to check everything off of the list that needed to be done and one thing that we always talked about was that the cake had to be amazing. It did not have to be the expensive over-the-op decorative cake, we just wanted to have a delicious one because we both agreed, that while they looked great, a lot of times wedding cakes do not taste great. Her aunt always made food for family get-togethers and we knew she made amazing cakes. Her aunt did not hesitate in agreeing to make our cake for us.

After checking all of the boxes off about the ceremony, we discussed where we wanted to go for a honeymoon. It was a no-brainer for both of us. Ashley was always a huge Disney fan and so was I. But there was also Universal Studios which had the Harry Potter theme park, and I was always a huge Harry Potter fan and still am to this day. So, it was decided, we couldn't resist planning to visit both theme parks.

Planning this trip was not easy as neither of us had ever been on this type of vacation before and never had planned one. Looking at the prices for everything, it quickly became apparent that the honeymoon was going to cost way more than the entire ceremony and reception combined. Despite that, Ashley and I both agreed that saving money on the wedding itself in order to have an amazing honeymoon experience, was well worth it.

The wedding was finally upon us and although exciting, stress levels were at an all-time high. Since the park was rented for only 2 days, we had to set everything up the day before with only a few hands to help. I think in situations like this, you can plan all you want but you will never be fully prepared. My lesson learned was that sometimes you just have to go with the flow and take things in stride.

Making anything exactly perfect is nearly impossible, but don't let striving for perfection ruin happy moments.

Overall, the day of the wedding itself is still kind of a blur to me. All of the stress of the setup and making sure things were going as smoothly as possible made time speed up. I started to think if I could have done more to make the decorations better or if I could have saved more money to make the whole thing more glamorous for Ashley. All I wanted was for her to be happy and get the wedding of her dreams. But once the ceremony started, all of those thoughts and insecurities melted away. Seeing the person you love to walk down the aisle on your wedding day is one of the few moments in life where time literally feels like it is standing still and you feel your heart stop. Although I did not cry myself, I understand why so many people do at this moment. For these brief few moments, everything was indeed, perfect.

After the ceremony, we had the reception immediately after. Spending time with her family on having Mary and Ed drive over 6 hours to attend, made it all more special. Once the night was over, we, unfortunately, had to do all of the clean-up immediately after. Much of which I had to do myself. We did not end up getting to leave until after midnight and had our plans to start our drive to Orland, Florida early the next morning. Needless to say, we were completely wiped by the time we got home and had to get as much sleep as possible to get ready for the all day of driving that was to come.

Waking up the next morning despite having to clean up the night before was still a great feeling. Marrying Ashley meant I was starting to build my family in the way that I chose to. Some people do not understand that having a blood relationship does not mean you have to consider them your family. Family is a much deeper relationship, and while blood may mean someone is family technically, one of my favorite quotes is that "Your friends are the family members that you choose". And Ashley was and still is my best friend.

The drive down to Orlando was not an easy one to do in one single day. But we were excited to see what that week would bring. While I had traveled on some vacations with Mary and Ed, there had never been one that I anticipated as much as this one. After twelve hours of driving we had finally made it to our hotel and were completely exhausted, but we knew it was going to be a great week.

Every day down there was exciting and tiring at the same time. We knew we might not get to come back down for a long time, so we tried to do and see as much as we could each day. Being prepared for trips and theme parks such as Disney and Universal is a must. Ashley and I most certainly were not prepared but after a couple of days figure it out. While there are theme parks all over the country, it is easy to say that no one can match the detail that these two put in. For me going through the Hogwarts castle at Universal was an experience every Harry Potter fan must do at least once in their lives. The way they made portraits come to life and actually look like real paintings were absolutely spectacular. Needless to say, I immediately wanted to come back, if not just for that experience alone. The entire week between Disney and Universal was overwhelming in the greatest way. We walked way too much and our feet hurt every night, but I was truly happy.

One thing was certain, I came to realize that by focusing on striving or a perfect life for a long time, it would have been easy to miss out and ruin perfect moments like those I experienced on my honeymoon. Focusing on these moments can change your perspective and shape your future in ways you cannot even imagine. Looking back on how we made the wedding and honeymoon happen has always helped me refocus when I struggle with how life is going. It took a lot of work to make it happen and to pay for it all ourselves. But some of the best things in life are the ones you have to work hard for and that you can look back to reflect on the journey it took to get there rather than it just being handed to you.

CHAPTER 20

Once we returned from our vacation, we quickly had to jump back into our work lives. While I enjoyed working with some really great people where I was, I was not making a great deal of money. I knew that if I wanted to be able to take care of my family and also be able to allow for things like vacations in the future, I was going to have to find a new job. Looking for a new job can be a scary thing especially when you have a fear of failure or instability. I had to push through both of these and take a risk. I contacted a temp agency and started my job search while I maintained my current job.

Within a week they told me they had a position that would be a great fit for me and my background but that it was a temp-to-hire agreement. This meant that after a few months, the company would have the opportunity to hire me full-time if they felt I deserved it. I have never been someone to shy away from proving myself and knew that I would work hard to impress the company. I embraced the possibility of the unknown and took the risk at a temp-to-hire position at one of the largest health insurance companies in the nation, Anthem, Inc. Now it was solely in my own hands to prove to myself and to this company that I was a great worker and that I was worthy of being hired. Being confident in my intelligence, my skills as a worker, and my ability to adapt quickly to different situations were never an issue for me. But being given the opportunity to excel was. The unknowns that come with a new job will always be scary, but taking ownership of my future was empowering.

After starting this new job, I was definitely on edge for a few weeks, which was to be expected with starting a new job. However, after those few weeks, I was in the swing of things and was catching on very quickly. Within a month or so the manager told me that they already planned on hiring me full-time as soon as they were able to. Being officially hired was a huge relief to know that my hard work was paying off and being an official employee came with a large salary increase which helped ease my mind at home too. Being good with money helped me get this far but now having my first job where I was truly making a living made me ecstatic. I could now afford to pay my bills, treat myself here and there and start building my savings up.

Within a couple months of being officially hired I was already being offered a promotion to become the primary trainer for my department. This was a huge step and spoke volumes as there were people that had been in the department for over 10 years and yet I proved that I was the right person for the job after only a few months. It appeared that everything that I was working for was actually happening.

Although work was going well at that time, outside of work I was dealing with some health issues. Over the years I had noted some lumps on my ribcage that were quite painful at the time. I had seen a few different doctors but nothing seemed to be happening to address the issue. One surgeon I had visited actually told me I was imagining the lumps and to not worry about it. As time went on after seeing that surgeon the lumps grew significantly bigger. It was pretty clear at this point that I was not imagining them. Finally, after going through so much pain and the lumps growing, I had seen another surgeon who agreed that agree to do surgery to remove them. It was a quick procedure with limited recovery time. Luckily, it turned out that they were merely lipomas, which is a fatty tissue mass that accumulates in the body. The issue was, that mine had burrowed in between my ribcage which was most likely what was causing me so much pain. The surgeon said he had to dig them out which may cause some scarring and continued pain. However, the pain wouldn't be anything close to what I was going through before. After years of dealing with this and having to be told I was crazy and just imagining things, it was a relief to have the surgery done and that it wasn't more serious than what it was.

Nearly a year had gone by being in my new position and after my surgery. I wanted to start working on myself more and more to work towards being healthier and enjoying life. I started working out to lose weight and was experiencing an unusual amount of pain from both of my shoulders. In high school, I had injured my right shoulder but never thought after so many years that I would still be having pain during workouts. It was clear that this was more than just soreness from a good workout. So once again I was going through the process of seeing a surgeon to try and figure out what was going on. Since I am right-handed, we decided to address my right should pain first. After the x-rays did not show any signs of damage, I had to start by going through physical therapy to try and strengthen the muscles and see if the pain continued. Unfortunately, this didn't help and we moved on to trying a cortisol shot. Again, it did not help. After all of this, the doctors decided to order an MRI; but once again there was no sign of damage. He then told me we were on our last resort. I either stop looking and hope the pain subsides, or he takes a scope and looks directly to see if there was any damage to my shoulder. At which point he could just perform the surgery then and there to repair it. It had been months of pain at this point, so despite the x-rays and MRI not showing any signs of damage, I chose the scope. Throughout my life, I had gone through nearly 20 surgeries by this point, so I was used to being put under with anesthesia, but I will never get used to the grogginess that comes with coming out of surgery. Once the surgery was done, the doctor confirmed that I had in fact had a torn labrum and that he had done the necessary repair. I was now going to have to go back to physical therapy to get my strength and range of motion back. It was going to be a long road to recovery but a much-needed one.

I was in physical therapy for many months but was eventually able to get back to almost normal. I never got the full range of motion back in my shoulder, but it beats the pain that I was experiencing when trying to lift things or work out. Nearly a year after the surgery on my right arm, I was still experiencing pain in my left arm. So once again, I had to go back to the doctor and start the process all over again. Just like on my right arm, the x-rays did not show any damage, trying to strengthen the muscles, and cortisol shots did nothing to ease the issues. Also, once again, the MRI did not show any damage. The doctor agreed to do the scope as he did on my other arm, and the surgery was scheduled.

After it was all said and done, he told me my left arm was actually worse than my right. I had had a torn labrum, a partially torn rotator cuff, and a torn bicep tendon. With having so much damage to my shoulders, which appeared to have been at the same time, he asked me how I could have done something like that. I had no idea, and couldn't think of any incident that would have caused it.

Despite already going through it once before, I was not ready to have to spend months in physical therapy again. This time around the therapists knew me and didn't even try to tell me what exercises to do. I just came in and was able to go through it by myself. When it was all over, I was hoping it would be my last for a long time.

CHAPTER 21

During the time of dealing with my second should surgery, Ashley and I had been making some big life decisions which made it even more important to get the surgery out of the way. Throughout this whole time of this surgery and physical therapy, Ashley and I had both discussed going back to school. She wanted to go back to get her Bachelor of Nursing Degree and I wanted to go back to get my Master of Business Administration. By now, we had also been married for two years and felt it was time to start a family. We were excited to be parents but knew that once our child came along there was no way that we could both be in school, working full-time, and raising a child. I made the decision to hold off on going back to school so that she could go to school first. It was going to take her about a year and a half to finish, so she wanted to get started right away.

About a month or so before she was set to start school, Ashley and I found out she was pregnant and couldn't be more excited. I always wanted to have children of my own one day and to give them a better life than I had. And now it was going to happen. With the way that everything fell our child was going to be born in December of 2016 and Ashley was going to be in school until December of 2017. This meant we were going to have to learn pretty quickly how to balance our schedules with her working night shift, going to school full time, and my working full time during the day. It was going to be challenging but we were ready to embrace it together.

Time was going by really fast and we were ready to find out if we were having a boy or a girl. In our discussions about wanting to start a family, Ashley and I had both agreed with eventually wanted to have two kids. One boy and one girl. After finding out the sex of our first child, all we truly cared about was knowing that they were healthy. Even with that being said, it was still exciting to find out. The day had come and we learned that we were having a baby boy. We already knew what name we were going with and were ready to start buying clothes and everything else. By the time he was going to be born, we were going to be ready.

The months leading up to the due date went by quickly and we were getting more excited to meet our son. It is hard to explain the love you feel for an unborn child. Many people without kids don't always understand, but once you experience it yourself it finally makes sense. Throughout her pregnancy, Ashley experienced a lot of sickness and I did anything I could to try and help. If anything, I was overly cautious as I didn't want her to have to lift anything or over-exert herself just to be safe. The whole time though, she still maintained her work schedule and was busting out her school work.

When December had finally arrived, I didn't know if we were fully prepared, but we were still ready to meet our son. The list of things to do before he was born kind of went out the window as time really did fly by. Baby-proofing the entire house and locking up cleaning supplies are small things that I easily just didn't think about enough. But now that things were so close, I started thinking about every little thing that had to be done.

As the due date really approaches, you start counting down the days. But after the due date came and Ashley wasn't in labor yet, it became about counting how many days after the due date it had been. One day, two days, three days, the days just kept going. It took nearly two weeks after the due date, and then it happened. Ashley and I were just hanging out watching tv and she realized her water had broken. Oddly enough I didn't freak out or anything. I was completely calm and helped get everything ready as it was finally time for the hospital.

Getting to the hospital, Ashley wasn't fully in labor yet so it was a slower process. Once we were checked in and the staff got us settled into our room. It was another waiting game. Time was ticking and as the hours went by, our son was still not ready to join the world. The doctors gave Ashley some medicine to help induce the labor and speed things along. Shortly after, she wasn't acting right and her vitals were clearly abnormal. Her heart rate was getting really low and it turned out she was having an adverse reaction to the medicine used for inducing labor. For the first time that day, I was starting to worry. The nurses and doctor were able to get her taken care of and back to normal but after her reaction to the medicine, they now had to make the decision to perform a C-section. Ashley wanted to go as naturally as possible, but that was just not possible at that point.

It didn't take long before they were ready to take us back to the room where the c-section was going to occur. I had gone through so many surgeries in my life and never really got scared. However, seeing Ashley have to go through something for the first time, I was petrified and didn't really know how to react. Knowing she was scared herself, I tried to not show any fear and just wanted to reassure her that everything was going to be alright. As we walked into the room, they had asked me if I wanted to watch or stand behind a curtain and just be near Ashley's head so she could see me. There was absolutely no way I was going to watch her be cut open.

Surprisingly enough, once it all started, it didn't take too long before they were finished. Our son was finally coming into the world. They took him out and I don't even remember him crying or screaming, but the doctors didn't seem worried so I knew he was okay. After they cleaned him off and wrapped him up, I got to hold him first. Holding him in my arms, he looked up at me and opened his eyes. I was immediately filled with overwhelming love. As I stated before, it is hard to explain the love one has for an unborn child. But once they are actually born is a whole new level of emotion. I knew from that moment on, that I had a true purpose in the world and that it was to be a great father and raise my child, Peyton James, in a home filled with happiness and love.

With having to have a c-section Ashley was going to have to stay in the hospital for a couple days, and I wasn't going to be leaving her there alone. We learned a lot really quickly about being new parents; between the feeding schedules and learning to change a diaper for a newborn was definitely new territory for both of us. After a couple days at the hospital, we were finally able to bring Peyton home. The first few weeks with him were definitely exhausting and exciting at the same time. Ashley of course had a lot to deal with so I continued to do everything I could to support her. Especially now that she was also adding surgery recovery on top of everything else.

Going back to work and getting back into the swing of things was challenging knowing that Ashley would be on her own throughout the day. I just wanted to be there for her as much as possible. One thing that helped was that she was able to take a couple months off of work for maternity leave. But she did not take any time off of school and just kept chipping away at her degree.

One thing I will say is that people always tell you about how much time flies by after school is over and other things like that and as a child or teenager you never believe it. Working full-time as an adult, time already goes by pretty quickly. However, after having a child, time speeds up exponentially. The first few weeks after they are born goes by in a blink of an eye. Before you know it, they are a month old, then six months old, starting to talk starting to walk, and then running. Every single milestone and each holiday becomes a bigger deal, and it makes you realize how we take we can these moments for granted.

Peyton's first birthday came up quickly which was exciting in itself. But this same month, Ashley was finally finished with all of her schooling and received her Bachelor's Degree in Nursing. She worked so hard being a mom, working full time on night shift and going to school full time and it finally paid off. After she was done, I moved right ahead with applying to grad school so that I could get my Master's Degree. With our work schedules, I too had to look for a school that I could complete online and on my own time. I was able to find the perfect school for me and was enrolled and able to start within a few months.

When I started it took some time to get used to being back in school after being out for six years, but I was pretty quick to adapt. I was so determined to knock out the school work and get my degree as I knew that it would be harder and harder as Peyton grew older. Since I was able to work at my own pace and the courses were done as soon as I completed the work, I flew through the classes. In less than six months I finished and passed all but two classes and was able to take a couple weeks off for the holidays around Thanksgiving, Christmas, and Peyton's second birthday. Being in school to get my Master's degree and Peyton turning two was a unique feeling. Seeing him grow so much and his personality blossoming made every hardship and life challenges over the years worth it.

The one thing that made it hard for him growing up so much was that he really only had one set of grandparents in his life on a regular basis. And that was Ashley's parents. With my dad being gone and never having a real and trusting relationship with my mom, he would never get to call them grandma and grandpa. I had kept in touch with my mom over the years but it always had to be at a distance. She would be clean and sober for a few months and then go back off the rails and I was just exhausted from the continuous drama from it. It always seemed like the only reason she or even my siblings would call me was when they needed something. Because I was successful and had a full-time job, they made me feel like I owed them something, and thus had to help them out. It took me a long time to realize that I need to push them out of my life almost entirely to get them to stop. Still, I keep in touch sometimes just to know where everyone is at. Unfortunately, most of the time I just fear that I am going to get another call that a family member has overdosed and passed away. Overtime I had to realize that some people never change and that it is okay to put myself first. And in the case of Peyton, I was putting him first and protecting him from my family. While he knows one of my siblings as uncle, he will never know my mom as grandma. Without having another set of grandparents around all of the time, as a parent I had to realize that I don't have the same support system that a normal family has. If I needed a night out or just to run errands without Peyton for some reason, if Ashley's parents weren't available, then it just couldn't happen.

While they live far away and aren't in his life every day, Mary and Ed gladly stepped in to be Peyton's second set of grandparents. He loves them, and they love him. Any time they are in town they make sure they visit him and it makes his whole day. Many people don't think about these everyday challenges like continuous family support while in college or what the dynamics look like when a foster youth has a child and they don't know who the child will call grandma and grandpa. I consider myself lucky with the people that are in Peyton's life, but at the same time, I wish there was more and that I had a bit more of a normal family life.

After the holidays and Peyton's second birthday party, I was ready to kick things back into gear and wrap up my last two college courses. So, I did just that. I ended up completing all of the work and passing my last two classes in about 6 six making my entire Master's Degree done in less than 7 months. When I finally received the results for my last class saying that I had passed, I cried. I was so relieved and happy I didn't really know what else to do. It was a huge weight off of my shoulders but it also filled me with a huge sense of accomplishment. Through years of hard work, patiently waiting, and wanting to go back to get my MBA, I had done it.

After the school had heard about my experience in foster care and completing my degree, I was asked to do an interview to share more about my story. I was given the opportunity to help share my story on the news as well which was a pretty awesome experience. I had a chance to show others what the possibilities were and that no matter what people tell you, you can accomplish your goals and achieve your dreams. Once again, I was proving that I, a former foster youth, was not just another statistic. And I was and am a success story.

Most of this time around graduating was a great experience, one thing came out of it. After my news story aired, my mom had reach out to me again. We were still in occasional contact at this point but after seeing the news she was not too happy and had to tell me why. In sharing my story, I always tell others about how my mom had abandoned us in a hotel room and that I was only ten years old at the time. In hearing this, she kept asking me why I hated her so much and why I still hold onto what she did in the past, and why I couldn't just forgive her.

The thing was that I had gotten over what she had done, I had forgiven her and moved on. But I did not forget what she had done, it was a huge part of my past and shaped my entire future. All of these things I could easily respond to her message to me. But then she said something that really angered me and helped me realize why I did not want her in my life regularly. After all of those questions, she began to state how she never abandoned my siblings and me. Her reasoning was that my older sister, who was only 15 at the time, was with us and had known what she was doing. And therefore, it did not count as abandonment.

At this point, I was done arguing and listening. There was no changing her anymore and I wasn't about to keep wasting my energy on someone who after 19 years couldn't admit to one of the biggest mistakes of her life. I was at a happy and exciting time in my life, and this brief moment of anger that my mom had caused was not going to change that. She did not have to admit to what she did and she probably never would. I am okay with that. With so many hateful moments in my life, getting to where I have in life, I realized there is no sense in hanging onto all of that hate or even responding to it. Hate will not add anything to your life, but love and kindness will not only shape your life but can shape and changes others' lives as well. And that is the legacy that I want for my life.

All of these moments and experiences have shaped me into who I am today. While no one should ever have to go through foster care or face the abuse and neglect that I did. I know had I had to go through everything that I did to become the man I was supposed to be. Instead of asking why did something have to happen to me, I have begun asking what did this moment teach me. This mentality has changed my life and brought forth a mindset of continuous growth and hope rather than that of resentment and despair. Even while in grad school and beyond, I have faced many challenges including identify theft, health issues, challenges at work, home damage, and more. But with everything I have been through and overcome, I know I can face each challenge head-on and come out on the other side even better.

CHAPTER 22

A lot of different things have attributed to my success today, and there are many people I have to thank. If you are in a similar situation as what I went through or just in a rough place in your life, always remember to keep your head up and look to the future. Do not let others keep you down and walk all over you. Also, if you are being abused or treated unfairly, speak up and say something. No one deserves to be abused or mistreated.

Do not be afraid to ask for help; you cannot do everything by yourself. I was homeless at times because I did not want to suck up my pride and say something to the ones who cared about me. Speak up and tell people what is going on in your life. Not everyone will lend a helping hand and do not expect them to. But you will never know who will help if you do not ask. You may be surprised at how much others are willing to help. Try to do whatever you can to improve your own lifestyle. Going to college can be rough, but it has bettered my life drastically and will help support my future. Not everyone goes to college or can afford to. I know that I had to use a mass amount of student loans to pay for college, but I did not let that stop me. Always keep fighting to better your life. Do not settle for the minimum in life and set low goals for yourself. Push yourself to be your best. As long as you try your best in everything that you do, you will never be a failure.

Another thing I would say to all of you is that sometimes you have to just take things as they come and sometimes you have to go one day at a time. But do not let that get you down. Keep pushing and fighting for what is right and what you want out of life. And lastly, do not be afraid to experience life. It is okay to have fun and enjoy life, but do know that fun does not have to include doing drugs or drinking and being irresponsible. Every time that I tell others about what I have been through I get asked the same question. "How is it that you made it through everything without becoming a hateful and mean person? And how have you been able to push through and get where you are today after all of that?" It is not the simplest of answers, but I just tell them you have to fight for what they believe in. Hope and strive for a better future. Do not expect anyone else to help you, sometimes you have to fight to make things better for yourself. It is a hard and lonely road at times, but if you push yourself and make it through. You will become that much of a better person for it. I do not care what anyone tells you. No matter what you go through in life you can get through it and become the person you want to be.

For me, going through all that I did in my life and coming out on the other side, I know it sometimes cannot be done alone. I feel that I have been called to give back to the foster care community and share my story and to fight for changes that are needed not only where I came from, but across the nation. I am going to continue to advocate for changes that give children who experience abuse the resources and trust they greatly need in life. And for children that experience foster care, I will fight to give them a sense of normalcy while in care and for them to have the resources and support they greatly need after leaving care. For many, once you turn 18 in the system, you are on your own and are kicked out on the streets. Being a child in foster care is not a choice and turning 18 should not put our lives in danger simply because were in foster care.

What does this mean for me and my future? I will never stop sharing my story. I count myself one of the lucky ones that went through the system and even though I didn't have the greatest overall experience and that says a lot about some of the change that needs to occur. I wrote my story to share this experience but to also show others that despite all of it, I am a success and they can be too. Because of my advocacy, I have already begun being asked to speak to former foster youth, lawmakers, and even in college classrooms and this is just the beginning. I hope to change foster care by working with lawmakers to build a better system. Maybe one day, I will even run for office myself. Sometimes we must stop asking for others to make a change for us, and instead take a stand and BE the change we want to see in the world.

Printed in the USA
CPSIA information can be obtained
at www.ICGtesting.com
JSHW011507221023
50603JS00014B/110

9 781088 289747